Introduction

In the United States, after the end of the 1914–18 war, aviation – military and civil alike – had slipped into the doldrums, mainly because of a steadfast refusal by Congress, under President Coolidge, to budget any funds for its development. Neither was there much incentive to develop new types of aircraft, as the market was flooded with thousands of surplus military machines, most of them in mint condition, and they were sold off to anyone who wanted them at ridiculously cheap prices.

As was also the case in Europe, the key to development in civil aviation during this period was mail. In 1925, Congress passed the Air Mail Act, which turned over the carriage of air mail to private contractors. There was already a coast-to-coast air mail route, which was flown by military aircraft on charter to the U.S. Post Office, but under the new Act bids were authorized for certain connections to this route. The most profitable and potentially worthwhile of these was the New York–Boston connection, for which there were two serious bidders: one was Eastern Air Transport, founded in September 1925 by Juan Trippe, and the other was Colonial Airlines, which was run by a consortium of influential investors. The two companies merged and became Colonial Air Transport, which was duly awarded the contract. In 1930, having acquired many more smaller operators, Colonial was developed into American Airways, later to be rebranded as American Airlines.

Meanwhile, in November 1925, another company called Western Air Express had been awarded a contract to carry mail between Los Angeles and Salt Lake City, beginning operations in April 1926 with six Douglas M-2 biplanes, conversions of military observation aircraft. In May 1926, Western Air Express began to carry passengers whenever the mail load permitted, the trip costing $90.

The carriage of passengers in addition to mail and freight was an attractive formula, and one adopted by the 'big four' U.S. airlines – Transcontinental & Western Air, American, United and Eastern – by 1930. At this time, the airlines were mainly equipped with two types of three-engine aircraft, the Fokker Trimotor, built by Fokker in the United States, and the Ford Trimotor. Although similar in configuration, there was one major difference between the two designs: the Fokker was of wooden construction, while the Ford was all metal.

On 31 March 1931, a Fokker F.10 Trimotor of TWA crashed in Kansas during a thunderstorm after a wing collapsed, killing all eight on board. The accident caused great concern throughout the United States, not least because one of the victims was Knute Rockne, a famous sportsman and coach of the renowned Notre Dame football team. Numerous factors complicated the subsequent investigation, resulting in difficulty establishing, with certainty, the cause of the crash. The investigation was initially undermined by a severe shortage of evidence: when government investigators first arrived at the crash site, they found that most of the wreckage had been taken by souvenir hunters and scavengers, leaving only engines, wings and propeller. Eventually, it was determined that the most likely cause of the accident, which possibly occurred in severe turbulence, was the composition of the aircraft. The wings of the Fokker Trimotor were made of wood laminate. In this instance, moisture had leaked into the interior of one wing over a period of time and had weakened the glue bonding the structure. One wing spar finally failed, causing the wing to develop uncontrolled flutter and separate from the aircraft.

As a consequence of this accident, all commercial aircraft of wooden construction were subjected to stringent and costly checks. All TWA's Fokker Trimotors were grounded, and later destroyed. TWA found itself in desperate need of a new airliner, and Jack Frye, the airline's Vice-President

The Ford Trimotor, seen here, and the Fokker Trimotor were the two principal types used by the embryo U.S. airlines in the 1920s and early 1930s. Unlike the Fokker type, the Ford airliner was of all-metal construction. (Langley Research Centre)

The Boeing Model 247, seen here in the livery of United Air Lines, was a successful design that seemed to have a promising future, but a fatal accident and the decision of TWA not to adopt it sealed its fate. (Boeing)

of Operations, drew up a requirement for an all-metal three-engine monoplane to be powered by engines of 500–550 hp, with a seating capacity of twelve passengers, a cruising speed of 150 mph, a maximum speed of at least 185 mph, landing speed not exceeding 65 mph, a service ceiling of at least 21,000 feet and a range of at least 1,080 miles. The aircraft would have to be able to take off on two engines from any airport served by the airline's transcontinental routes, including 'hot and high' locations such as the 4,954-feet-high airfield at Albuquerque, New Mexico, where temperatures frequently exceeded 90°F or 32°C.

One airliner then being developed would have fitted the requirement admirably, except that it had two engines instead of three. This was the Boeing Model 247, an aircraft intended to revolutionize air transport. The Boeing 247 prototype, which was designed to carry ten passengers and a crew consisting of pilot, co-pilot and stewardess, made its maiden flight on 8 February 1933, and immediately made the entire world of commercial aircraft seem obsolete. Like its B-9 military bomber precursor, the new aircraft had an all-metal structure and was a low-wing monoplane with a retractable undercarriage. It was very streamlined, had good all-round performance and low operating costs, and its technical innovations included a wing and tail de-icing system. However, United Air Lines had a complete monopoly of the 247 production line, having invested the then fantastic sum of $3.5 million in an order for sixty aircraft before the prototype had even flown, and Boeing Air Transport, which was part of the United Group, introduced the first 247 into service on 30 March 1933.

Not only did the 247 cut eight hours off the transcontinental service, it also combined speed with a high standard of comfort. In its first month of service, it brought United a massive increase in ticket sales. Then, on 10 October 1933, a 247 bound for Chicago exploded in mid-air over Indiana, killing all seven on board. The aircraft was not at fault – the disaster had been caused by an explosive item of cargo that had found its way on board – but the aircraft inevitably lost some of its passenger appeal as a result. Nevertheless, its future might have been assured if Boeing had been in a position to sell it to TWA, which wanted it badly; but at that time both Boeing and United were still controlled by the same board of directors, and they turned down TWA's application.

Meanwhile, on 2 August 1932, Jack Frye had circulated TWA's requirement to five other U.S. aircraft manufacturers – Consolidated, Curtiss, Douglas, General Aviation and Martin – and ten days later representatives of the Douglas Aircraft Company in Santa Monica, California, presented their proposal for a new all-metal, twin-engine airliner design called the Douglas Commercial One, or DC-1. After several weeks of intensive negotiations Douglas convinced Jack Frye that the DC-1 could meet or even exceed all of TWA's requirements, and on 20 September 1932 TWA contracted to buy the first DC-1 for $125,000, with options on a further sixty aircraft at a unit cost of $58,000, minus engines.

From that moment on, although Boeing's name would become a synonym for long-range air transport, it would be Douglas machines that would dominate the domestic routes of the United States, and of half the world.

Douglas DC-1 and DC-2

Only one DC-1 was built. Powered by two 690-hp Wright SGR-1820F3 Cyclone air-cooled radial engines fitted with three-blade variable-pitch metal propellers, it flew for the first time on 1 July 1933 from Clover Field, Santa Monica, with Douglas chief test pilot Carl Cover at the controls. The passenger cabin was insulated against noise, fully heated, and the aircraft was capable of flying and performing a controlled take-off or landing on one engine. During six months of testing, the DC-1 made more than 200 test flights and demonstrated its clear superiority over both the Fokker Trimotor and Ford Trimotor. On 19 February 1934 it flew across the United States in a record time of thirteen hours, five minutes.

The DC-1 was accepted into TWA service on 15 September 1933 and was subsequently used mainly as a test vehicle, although a few commercial flights were also made. Meanwhile, Douglas had made some improvements to the basic design, installing more powerful 710-hp Wright Cyclone engines and increasing the seating capacity to fourteen. The modified airliner, designated DC-2, had a fuselage two feet longer than that of the DC-1 in order to accommodate the two extra passengers. It was a low-wing monoplane of all-metal construction, featuring a cantilever wing and a semi-monocoque fuselage using Douglas-Northrop cellular multi-web construction with parallel chord centre section built integrally with the fuselage. The cantilever tail surfaces were also of multi-cellular construction. The two main wheels, when retracted, protruded from the engine nacelles to minimize damage to the aircraft's undersurfaces in the event of a wheels-up landing.

The passenger seats in the main cabin could be adjusted and rested on rubber mounts to minimize vibration. Forward of the passenger seating, and in line with the engines, a compartment accommodated up to 1,000 lb of freight and mail, while another compartment immediately aft of the flight deck held luggage and extra cargo. Entry to the passenger cabin was through a single door in the port side of the fuselage; there was a small buffet area to the rear of the door, and toilet facilities were provided at the rear of the cabin.

TWA's first DC-2, named *City of Chicago*, made its maiden flight on 11 May 1934 and was delivered to the airline three days later. TWA's brochure was lavish in its praise of its so-called 'Sky Queen':

'The silver ship is a low-wing cantilever monoplane. The entire external appearance

Only one Douglas DC-1 was built, but from the outset it showed a clear superiority over the trimotor designs then in use. The DC-1 was accepted into TWA service on 15 September 1933 and was subsequently used mainly as a test vehicle, although a few commercial flights were also made.

of the transport is remarkable for its complete freedom from struts and control system parts. In harmony with clean design, the wheels retract into the engine nacelles... The passenger salon is 26 ft 4 in long, 5 ft 6 in wide and 6 ft 3 in high. The great height of the passenger salon permits even the tallest person to walk fully erect in the cabin for its entire length. The compartment is fitted to accommodate 14 passengers in two rows of specially-designed lounge chairs 40 in wide and separated by an aisle 16 in wide. Chairs are deeply upholstered and fully adjustable for reclining or reversing to face the passenger behind. Each seat has a private window and because of the height of the seat above the wing there is excellent vision from all chairs... Flying in the new

Passenger comfort, DC-2 style. Passengers on board a TWA DC-2 enjoy a buffet meal. The standard of service was remarkable for its time.

TWA's first DC-2, named *City of Chicago*, made its maiden flight on 11 May 1934 and was delivered to the airline three days later. TWA's inaugural service with the DC-2 was launched on 18 May 1934. (TWA)

The modern, streamlined configuration of the DC-2 is apparent in this excellent image. (Source unknown)

Mail and freight being loaded onto a DC-2 of Pan American Grace Airways (Panagra). (PanAm)

luxury liner transport is like putting wings on a luxurious living room and soaring in complete security and comfort. The Douglas transport is the crowning achievement in commercial transportation, creating a new ideal in luxurious travel combined with high-speed and high-performance characteristics coupled with great security.'

TWA's inaugural service with the DC-2 was launched on 18 May 1934, the aircraft flying on the Columbus, Ohio-Pittsburgh, Pennsylvania–Newark and New Jersey route sectors. A week later the aircraft began serving Chicago and Newark, breaking the speed record between the two cities four times in one eight-day period. A transcontinental service, named Sky Chief, operated from New York to Los Angeles by way of Chicago, Kansas City and Albuquerque; the flight took sixteen hours and twenty minutes eastbound and eighteen hours westbound, considerably faster than the Boeing 247s of TWA's rival, United Air Lines.

Eventually, TWA acquired twenty DC-2s. Further orders followed quickly from other airlines. Eastern Air Lines placed an order for fourteen aircraft to serve their east coast routes to Miami, Florida; fourteen more in total were ordered by American and Pan American Grace (Panagra); Pan American Airlines ordered sixteen; and General Airlines (later Western Airlines) four. To promote Eastern's Miami service, the company's general manager and America's leading air ace of the First World War, Captain Eddie Rickenbacker, organized a one-day VIP excursion between New York and Miami, treating his guests to dinner in the latter city and returning them to New York the same day.

The DC-2 found a ready market in the Netherlands, which had enjoyed two major advantages when it came to founding the basis of a civil aviation network in the post-war years. One was Anthony Fokker, designer of the renowned range of combat aircraft that had equipped the German Flying Corps; the second was a young lieutenant in the Dutch Army Aviation Service named Albert Plesman. In the

The Oklahoma City-based trunk carrier Braniff opersated seven DC-2s, all purchased from TWA When the latter acquired the DC-3. Two examples are seen here, alongside the airline's Lockheed Electras.

summer of 1919, Plesman, together with another lieutenant, M. Hofstee, organized a very successful aircraft exhibition in Amsterdam. The interest shown by people concerned with aviation from all over Europe encouraged Fokker, who had lost everything following Germany's collapse, to form a new company, while Albert Plesman toured Holland's business world and set about raising funds to establish a Dutch civil airline. On 7 October 1919, having secured sufficient backing, the new airline was registered at The Hague. Its title was Koninklijke Luchtvaart Maatschappij NV (Royal Dutch Airlines, abbreviated to KLM), the 'Royal' having been granted by HM Queen Wilhelmina as a token of her confidence in the airline's future.

Throughout the 1920s KLM relied on the series of commercial airliners developed by Anthony Fokker, reliable aircraft that were in use by airlines throughout the world, but by the end of 1932 Albert Plesman, KLM's co-founder, was searching for a new and ultra-modern airliner that would serve KLM on both the European and Far Eastern routes until well into the 1940s.

Albert Plesman was in no doubt that the DC-2 would be the ideal vehicle for KLM's Far East service, offering a new dimension in speed and passenger comfort, and in November 1933 he made the first move to obtain licence rights from Douglas to manufacture the DC-2 in Holland, although it was by no means clear who the Dutch manufacturer would be. However, Anthony Fokker, sensing which way the wind was blowing, made his own approach to Douglas, narrowly beating Plesman's bid. The outcome was that Fokker Aircraft became the manufacturing and sales agent for the DC-2 (and also, later, for the DC-3) in Europe. Fokker ultimately went on to sell thirty-nine DC-2s to various customers, although none of the new airliners was in fact built in Holland. Although Fokker had acquired a production licence from Douglas

for $100,000, aircraft destined for KLM and other European customers were built and air-tested by Douglas in the U.S., then shipped by sea with wings and propellers detached, then re-assembled by Fokker at airfields near Cherbourg or Rotterdam, the ports of debarkation. Plans were also made to manufacture the DC-2 under licence by Airspeed Ltd in Britain, but this deal was never closed.

The first DC-2 acquired by KLM was PH-AJW *Uiver* (Stork), which joined the fleet in August 1934 and, in October, took part in the MacRobertson Air Race from RAF Mildenhall in Suffolk to Melbourne. The aircraft captain on this flight was K.D. Parmentier, with Jan Moll as first officer and B. Prins as flight engineer, and three fare-paying passengers were also carried, in addition to 30,000 airmail letters. Out of twenty entrants, it finished second only behind the purpose-built de Havilland DH.88 Comet racer *Grosvenor House*. During the total journey time of ninety hours, thirteen minutes, the DC-2 was in the air for eighty-one hours, ten minutes, and won the handicap section of the race. (The DH.88 finished first in the handicap section, but race regulations permitted the crew to claim only one victory.) The DC-2 followed KLM's regular 9,000-mile route, 1,000 miles longer than the official race route, carrying mail, making every scheduled passenger stop, turning back once to pick up a stranded passenger, and even becoming lost in a thunderstorm. It also briefly got bogged down in mud after a diversionary landing at Albury racecourse on the very last leg of the journey.

This DC-2 *Uiver*'s career with KLM was destined to be short, however, for it crashed at Rutbah in Iraq on 20 December 1934 with the loss of all seven passengers and crew. KLM's second DC-2, PH-AKG *Gaai*, was also unfortunate; entering service with the airline on 30 March 1935, it crashed in bad weather on landing at Piah San

Giacomo on 20 July that same year, killing all thirteen souls on board.

Despite the loss of its first DC-2, KLM ordered nineteen more aircraft in April and May 1935, and some of these were pressed into service on the Amsterdam–Djakarta route, reducing the flight time to fifty-seven hours. Their debut enabled KLM to combine passengers and mail satisfactorily and, in fact, began to deprive Britain's Imperial Airways of much business along the route sectors extending to Singapore.

In July 1935, three DC-2s (PK-AFJ, PK-AFK and PK-AFL) were purchased by the airline Koninklijke Nederlandsch-Indische Luchtvaart Maatschappij (Royal Dutch Indies Airways, KNILM), which despite its similar name was not a subsidiary of the better-known KLM. This airline, established in 1928, served the Dutch East Indies and,

DC-2 PH-AJW *Uiver* pictured at Darwin after the MacRobertson Air Race. PH-AJW was the first DC-2 acquired by KLM, joining the fleet in August 1934. (KLM)

Three DH.66 Comet racers were entered in the MacRobertson air race. The aircraft nearest the camera is G-ACSP *Black Magic*, in black and gold livery. Flown by Jim and Amy Mollison, it had to pull out when a piston seized as the result of using contaminated fuel. (BAe Systems)

Douglas DC-2 PH-AJU of KLM, the Royal Netherlands Airline. (KLM)

later, parts of Southeast Asia and Australia. The introduction of the DC-2 led to strong competition with the Qantas-Imperial Airways service from Darwin to Singapore, flying between Djakarta and Singapore and effectively reducing the flying time from seven hours to four.

In 1936, KNILM opened a new service with its DC-2s from Djakarta to Borneo; it was originally planned to extend this service to Manila, but this scheme was abandoned because of difficulties encountered in negotiations with the Philippine and U.S. governments. KLM also acquired its first DC-3 in that year; this was PH-ALI *Ibis*, which joined the fleet in October 1936. It was joined by thirteen more in 1937, three more in 1938 and a further five in 1939. A DC-3 service to Djakarta was begun in October 1937, reducing the flight time from fifty-seven to fifty-five hours.

Other customers for the DC-2 included Amtorg, the Soviet purchasing organization, which received one; Australian National Airways (two); the Austrian government (one); Avio Linee Italiane (one); China (six, operated by CNAC and Canton Airlines); CLS in Czechoslovakia (five); Deutsche Luft Hansa (one); the French government (one); Holyman's Airways in Australia (two); Iberia (one); Japan (six); LAPE (Líneas Aéreas Postales Españolas) in Spain (five); the Polish airline LOT (two); and Swissair (four). Some of the Swissair DC-2s had been sold on by other operators; these included HB-ISA, acquired in April 1936 after serving for eighteen months as the personal transport of Austria's president. It was later sold to Iberia as EC-EBB, then served with the Spanish Air Force. Another former Swissair DC-2, HB-ISA, originally built as PH-AKF, and then acquired by Spain, suffered a similar fate. Other Swissair DC-2s were HB-ITA, lost in a crash at Senlis, Paris, on 7 January 1939; HB-ITE, delivered in January 1935 and later sold to Phoenix Airlines in South Africa as ZS-DFW; HB-ITI,

which crashed at Dübendorf Zurich, on 28 February 1936; and HB-ITO, which was also sold on to Phoenix Airlines as ZS-DFX and later acquired by the French Company Air Nautic as F-BJHR. In Swissair service, the DC-2 inaugurated the Zurich–Basle–London air service, the 450-mile stage from Basle to London being probably the longest regular non-stop schedule in Europe.

On 27 March, 1934, Nakajima Hikoki K.K. acquired for the sum of $80,000 the licence rights to build the DC-2, and to sell the airliner in the Empire of Japan and Manchukuo. While the DC-2 design was being adapted to conform with Japanese production methods, one Douglas-built DC-2 was imported by Nihon Koku K.K. (Japan Air Transport Co Ltd), this aircraft being delivered in December 1934. Production of the DC-2 in Japan was started in 1935, the first aircraft, assembled from imported components and powered by two Wright Cyclone SGR-1820-F2 radial engines, making its first flight in February 1936. Five more aircraft, initially powered by SGR-1820-F2s but later re-engined with SGR-1820-F52s, were

Top: SP-ASI was one of a pair of DC-2s acquired by the Polish airline LOT. (LOT)

Above: A Japanese DC-2 seen in U.S. markings at Zamboanga in the Philippines after the Japanese surrender in 1945. (U.S. Army)

built by Nakajima in 1936/7 and delivered to Nihon Koku K.K. for operations on the airline's Japan–Formosa service. During the Pacific War the DC-2 was allocated the Allied code-name Tess in the belief that the aircraft was in widespread service with the Imperial Japanese Navy. In fact, only the first aircraft, assembled by Nakajima from imported Douglas-built components, was impressed into military service, and that was with the Imperial Japanese Army.

Just over a year after the DC-2 made its inaugural flight with TWA, the number of aircraft in service with twenty-one customers had risen to 108, logging a total of 20 million miles. A survey commissioned by Douglas revealed that 'United States operators and Pan American Airways in South America report 15,000,000 miles flown in the first eight months at an efficiency of 98.8 per cent... Of the 26,259,665 miles flown in the U.S. during the first six months this year, 7,286,437 were flown by Douglas transports, or 27.7 per cent. However, the 42 Douglas aircraft available for service constituted only 7.6 per cent of the total (commercial) airplanes in service in the U.S. – a remarkable tribute to the Douglas operating ability.'

Comfort, speed and, above all else, safety, were keywords that assured the success of the DC-2. Memories were still fresh of the disasters that had dogged commercial aviation in the U.S. during the previous decade. In 1926 and 1927 there had been a total of twenty-four fatal commercial airline crashes, a further sixteen in 1928, and fifty-one in 1929 (killing sixty-one), which remains the worst year on record at an accident rate of about one for every 1,000,000 miles (1,600,000 kilometres) flown. By the mid-1930s improved technology, including more effective navigation aids to route flying in bad weather, had made routine commercial aviation much more reliable. Nevertheless, the introduction of the DC-2 came at a cost. Between December 1934 and March 1939, twenty-one DC-2s were involved in fatal accidents, almost all of them due to bad weather or pilot error. Confidence in the aircraft itself remained high.

Douglas DC-3 in Detail

Even before the DC-2 had become firmly and effectively embedded in commercial service in the U.S. and Europe, a requirement had been identified for a more advanced, higher-capacity development that could generate profitable revenue by the carriage of passengers alone.

The prime movers in formulating the requirement were Cyrus Rowlett Smith, President of American Airlines, and William Littlewood, American Airlines' Vice-President of Engineering. Both men had flown in the DC-2 and had identified what they considered to be some shortcomings, the most serious of which was a lack of power. Flight test reports revealed that it could be difficult to land under certain conditions, and both aileron and rudder control needed to be much lighter. In the latter case, it was considered that an increase in fin area would solve the problem.

After spending hours on the telephone to Donald Douglas, who was reluctant to launch into a major redesign project which would divert resources away from the massively successful DC-2, Smith convinced Douglas that the way ahead was to design a 'sleeper' aircraft to augment and eventually replace the airline's twenty-one Curtiss Condor twelve-passenger luxury night sleeper transports, which were fitted with sleeper berths and capable of cruising at 190 mph, which was fast for a large biplane design. In the mid-1930s, American's Condors were making daily overnight flights between Dallas and Los Angeles, staging through Fort Worth, Abilene, Big Spring, El Paso, Douglas, Tucson, and Phoenix. The Condor was also in service with Eastern Air Lines.

In their negotiations, Smith and Douglas agreed that the new sleeper transport would use at least 80 per cent of the DC-2's components, but there was a compromise: Douglas agreed to go ahead, but only after Smith agreed to purchase twenty aircraft.

Work on the new airliner, known as the Douglas Sleeper Transport (DST) proceeded under the leadership of Arthur E. Raymond, Douglas's chief engineer. Despite the fact that there were many detail changes, the overall shape of the aircraft remained much the same, although the length of the fuselage and the wingspan were increased. The diameter of the fuselage was increased from 66 inches in the DC-2 to 92 inches, the tail was enlarged, a heavier undercarriage installed and foot-operated wheel brakes fitted. Despite the earlier agreement, the many design changes meant that there was in fact little commonality between

A Douglas Sleeper Transport of United Air Lines. The initial layout had seven upper and seven lower berths, with a separate private cabin up front for honeymoon couples.

the DST and its DC-2 predecessor, only about 10 per cent of the components being interchangeable. For one thing, the DST's fuselage cross-section was almost circular, so that stresses were evenly distributed throughout, whereas the DC-2's fuselage design had been box-like, with straight vertical walls supporting horizontal roof and floor. Also, the wings used a new multi-cellular stressed-skin construction, where the traditional main support beans (wing spars) and cross-members (ribs) were replaced with a honeycomb of strong metal boxes, riveted together to provide exceptional strength.

The first DST flew on 17 December 1935, its Wright Cyclone engines having been extensively run-up on the previous two days. The pilot on that maiden flight from Clover Field (now Santa Monica) was Carl A. Cover, who had flown the DC-1 when it first took to the air. He was accompanied by engineers Fred Stineman and Frank Collbohm, the latter acting as co-pilot. Take-off was at 3 pm and the aircraft touched down at 4.40 pm after an uneventful flight.

The first DST was retained by Douglas and underwent several months of flight testing before being accepted into service by American Airlines on 29 April 1936 as NC14988 'Flagship Texas'. Seven more production aircraft followed; the aircraft was originally fitted with fourteen to sixteen sleeping berths, but these were soon deleted and replaced by twenty-one seats, in which configuration it was given the designation DC-3. In total, forty DSTs were built before production ended in 1941.

In designing the DC-3, much thought had been given to passenger comfort. Douglas adopted a similar style of seating to that used in the luxury railway coaches of the Pullman Company. The passenger cabin was soundproofed thanks to its padded walls, carpeted floors, upholstered seats, rubber vibration dampers and shock absorbers, all of which combined to reduce vibration and in-flight noise. The aircraft featured a fresh-air ventilation system in which outside air was drawn through inlets fitted forward of the engine exhausts. There

The Douglas Sleeper Transport had a two-tier configuration. The windows giving the upper-tier passengers a view on the outside world are visible in this image. (National Air and Space Museum)

Douglas DST 'Flagship Skysleeper' of American Airlines with a Goodyear 'blimp' advertising the firm's famous tyres overhead. (DST Archive)

was consequently no need to open window panels to permit ventilation, as was the case in older airliners, which admitted engine exhaust fumes as well as outside air; the DC-3 flew with its windows closed, cutting out the deafening noise of slipstream and engines.

The design of the DC-3 was so excellent that the basic specifications for the aircraft remained unchanged throughout its long career, a rare phenomenon in the world of aviation.

A stewardess serving breakfast to the occupant of a sleeper berth on a United Air Lines Douglas DST. (DST Archive)

The luxurious DC-3 interior, with seats based on those installed in Pullman railway coaches.

low-altitude turbulence that caused much airsickness misery among the passengers of earlier airliners, and in hot conditions it could climb into cooler air, reducing cabin temperature by several degrees. Cabin pressurization, with its associated air conditioning, was still some years in the future. The Boeing 307 airliner of 1938 was the first airliner to feature a pressurized cabin, but only ten examples were built.

A further inducement to fly in the DC-3 was the provision of hot in-flight meals of a gourmet standard. American's 'Flagship Mercury' service from Newark, New Jersey, to Los Angeles, California, offered three breakfast and dinner menus served on genuine Syracuse china with Reed and Barton silverware. Wild rice pancakes with blueberry syrup, cheese omelettes, or Julienne of Ham omelette were the breakfast choices. For dinner there was Chicken Kiev, Long Island Duckling with Orange sauce, Breast of Chicken Jeanette, Strip Sirloin, or Filet Mignon, a choice of salads, and pastries for dessert. Lunch offered a lighter choice with consommé, fried chicken, peas, and mashed potatoes. Desserts included ice-cream, and chocolate sundaes. A flight attendant could serve twenty-one passengers in just over an hour.

There were other innovations. An automatic pilot, recently developed by the Sperry Gyroscope Company, was installed as standard equipment, and the cockpit featured two sets of instruments, so that if one set failed for any reason the other was there as backup. Instrument lighting was also incorporated, as night passenger services were to be a regular feature.

The first American Airlines DC-3 entered service on 7 June 1936 on the non-stop New York to Chicago route. American went on to acquire twenty-two more DC-3s before 1941, and its total fleet eventually rose to sixty-six. On 1 July 1936, three years to the day after the DC-1 first flew, President Franklin D. Roosevelt presented Donald W. Douglas with the Collier Trophy, awarded annually in recognition of the greatest achievement in aeronautics in the U.S. The presidential script related that 'This airplane, by reason of its high speed, economy, and quiet passenger comfort, has been generally adopted by transport lines throughout the United States. Its merit has been further recognized by its adoption abroad, and its influence on foreign design is already apparent. In making this award, recognition is given to the technical and production personnel of the Douglas organization.'

As though to underpin the DC-3's potential, it was announced on that same day that an American Airlines DC-3 had flown non-stop from Newark to Chicago and back, 1,472 miles, in just over eight hours, paving the way for a non-stop weekly service between the two cities.

Meanwhile, the popularity of the DC-3 rapidly generated orders from other major

Passenger comfort was further enhanced by the addition of a door in the starboard side of the fuselage. Passengers could now enter the aircraft without being buffeted by slipstream from the port engine, which was always started up first, as they embarked. The door in the port side was retained for the loading of luggage. Also, the performance of the aircraft itself provided a much smoother ride than had hitherto been possible. The DC-3 could climb above

A striking photograph of a DC-3 with both engines turning. Note the unlocked tailwheel, which would be locked when the aircraft was lined up for take-off on the runway. (Jud McCranie)

A DC-3 of Eastern Air Lines 'The Great Silver Fleet' pictured at the moment of touchdown. (NASM)

U.S. airlines, starting with United Air Lines, which became the second-largest DC-3 operator with forty-five aircraft and began its DC-3 services in June 1937. Other U.S. customers for the DC-3 included Braniff (10); Delta (6); Eastern (31); Hawaiian (3); Northeast (2); Northwest (11); Pan American (20); Panagra (12); Pennsylvania-Central (15); TWA (31); and Western (5).

Within three years of its introduction, the DC-3 accounted for 95 per cent of all commercial air traffic in the U.S. From commencement of service to the Japanese attack on Pearl Harbor, the DC-3 increased domestic revenue passenger miles more than fivefold. By the end of 1938, the 350th aircraft had been delivered, and of the 322 aircraft operated by the country's airlines in December 1941, 260 were DC-3s.

At the pre-war peak, thirty foreign airlines operated the DC-3. On the eve of war, the aircraft's scheduled flights represented 90 per cent of international air traffic.

Civil DC-3 production ended in 1942 after 607 aircraft had been built, and with America now in the war the Douglas production lines turned to the manufacture of military versions, the C-47 Skytrain and the U.S. Navy's R4D. More than 10,000

A DC-3 of Braniff International Airways. This photograph was taken after the war (John Proctor/Jetphotos)

were built and were used by the armed forces of many countries, the RAF and Commonwealth air forces naming the type Dakota. Including the versions built in the USSR and Japan, production rose to over 16,000.

DC-3 Characteristics
Crew: 2
Capacity: 21-32 passengers
Length: 64 ft 8 in (19.7 m)

DC-3 *Mauna Loa* of Hawaiian Airlines pictured over the Hawaiian Islands, probably in the 1950s. The first DC-3s were added to the fleet in August 1941, some remaining in service until their retirement in November 1968. (NASM)

Douglas DC-3 N25656 of Delta Air Lines. (NASM)

United Air Lines DC-3 NC16072 Mainliner. (NASM)

Wingspan: 95 ft 2 in (29.0 m)
Height: 16 ft 11 in (5.16 m)
Wing area: 987 sq ft (91.7 m²)
Empty weight: 16,865 lb (7,650 kg)
Gross weight: 25,200 lb (11,431 kg)
Fuel capacity: 822 gal (3,736 l)
Powerplant: Two Pratt & Whitney R-1830-S1C3G Twin Wasp 14-cylinder air-cooled two-row piston engines, 1,200 hp each
Propellers: 3-bladed Hamilton Standard 23E50 series, 11 ft 6 in (3.51 m) diameter

Performance
Maximum speed: 230 mph (370 kph) at 8,500 ft (2,590 m)
Cruise speed: 207 mph (333 kph)
Stall speed: 67 mph (108 kph)
Service ceiling: 23,200 ft (7,100 m)
Rate of climb: 1,130 ft/min (5.7 m/s)
Wing loading: 25.5 lb/ft² (125 kg/m²)

A Choice of Engines
The DSTs and early production DC-3s were powered by two air-cooled, supercharged Wright Aeronautical Division Cyclone 9 GR-1820G2 nine-cylinder radial engines, rated at 700 horsepower at 2,100 rpm for normal cruise and 800 horsepower at 2,100 rpm for take-off. They were fitted with three-bladed Hamilton Standard Hydromatic constant-speed propellers with a diameter of 11 ft 6 in (3.505 m). These engines were soon changed to more powerful air-cooled, supercharged Pratt & Whitney Twin Wasp SC3-G 14-cylinder radials, with a normal power rating of 950 horsepower at 2,550 rpm and take-off power rating of 1,050 horsepower at 2,700 rpm.

Foreign airlines, too, were quick to grasp the potential of the DC-3, starting with KLM, which ordered twenty-four aircraft to become the first European operator. Other foreign customers included AB Aerotransport of Sweden (5); Air France (1); Australian National Airways (4); Canadian Colonial Airways (4); LAV of Venezuela; the Polish airline LOT; Malert of Hungary; LARES of Romania; Panair do Brasil; Sabena of Belgium (2); and Swissair (5).

On 11 April 1936, following the purchase of a single DC-2 for evaluation in 1935, the Soviet government placed an order for eighteen DC-3s (later increased to twenty-one) for operation by the Soviet state airline, Aeroflot. The aircraft was to be produced under licence by Factory 84 (GAZ-84) at Moscow-Khimki, and designation PS-84 – Passazhirsk Samolyot 84 or Passenger Aircraft 84 – was allocated to it. The construction programme was directed by aeronautical engineer Boris Pavlovich Lisunov, who spent two and a half years between November 1936 and April 1939 with the Douglas Aircraft Company. He was accompanied by a team of engineers that included Vladimir Myasishchev, who would go on to design the USSR's Mya-4 jet bomber in the 1950s.

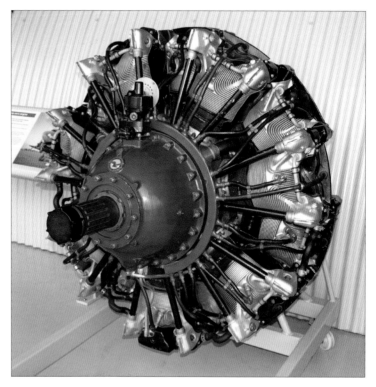

Above: The Pratt & Whitney Twin Wasp, seen here on display at the Imperial War Museum, Duxford, was used in over thirty different types of aircraft. A total of 173,618 R-1830 engines were built.

Left: One of Panair do Brasil's fleet of DC-3s. The airline had previously operated Sikorsky S.42 flying boats before reverting to landplanes.

Above: PH-ALI *Ibis* was the first DC-3 to serve with the Royal Dutch Airline. In 1943, taken over by BOAC and re-registered G-AGBB, it was shot down by German fighters over the Bay of Biscay.

Centre: A DC-3 operated by the Polish airline LOT.

LOT DC-3 SP-LCC. A refurbished C-47A, it was damaged beyond repair in March 1950 at an unknown location in Poland.

A DC-3 of Pacific Northwest Airlines pictured against a rugged and picturesque Alaskan background. The airline's main operating base was Anchorage.

A fine study of XA-FEG, one of Mexicana's fleet of DC-3s.

Below: LOT's SP-LKI was originally a Lisunov Li-2P.

Myasishchev was mainly responsible for incorporating many design changes to the original DC-3 drawings in order to conform to Soviet requirements. These eventually ran to 1,293 items, some involving major changes such as the installation of the Shvetsov Ash-62IR, a Soviet development of the 9-cylinder Wright R-1820 Cyclone 9. The latter engine was also used in the early 21-seat versions of the DC-3. The PS-84 also incorporated a slightly shorter span and the passenger door was moved to the starboard side of the fuselage, being replaced on the port side by a cargo door. Structural reinforcement included slightly heavier skins, because the metric skin gauges were not exact duplicates of the American alloy sheet metal. Standard Soviet metric hardware was different and the various steel substructures such as engine mounts and landing gear, wheels and tyres were also quite different from those of the original design. Later modifications allowed the provision of ski landing gear in order to operate in remote and Arctic regions.

The first PS-84s had begun to emerge from the GAZ-84 production line in 1939 and by the time Germany invaded the Soviet Union in June 1941, 237 PS-84s had been produced, all in civilian passenger configuration. Production was also undertaken by GAZ-33 at Tashkent, GAZ-124 at Kazan and GAZ-126 at Komsomolsk-on-Amur. Following on from the German invasion many of Aeroflot's PS-84s were impressed into military service, provided with a dorsal gun turret and re-designated Lisunov Li-2.

In total, the Soviet factories produced 4,937 Li-2s in many variants, its roles including airliner and freighter, as well as military transport, reconnaissance, aerial photography, parachute dropping, bomber and crop-spraying.

Japanese interest in the DC-3 was awakened in 1937 when two trading companies, the Mitsui Trading Company Ltd and the Far Eastern Trading Company Ltd, began placing orders for thirteen Cyclone-powered and seven Twin Wasp-powered DC-3s, the aircraft being delivered between November 1937 and February 1939. The DC-3s were operated by Dai Nippon Koku K.K. (Greater Japan Air Lines) and, less attritions through operational and combat losses, remained in service until the end of the Pacific War, when the survivors were scrapped.

From September 1940, huge numbers of DC-3s were ordered for the U.S. Army Air Corps (as the C-47 and C-53s) and U.S. Navy (as the R4D-1). Many civilian DC-3s were also impressed into military service and designated C-48 to C-52 inclusive. Many more were supplied to the Royal Air Force, in which they were known as the Dakota, and to other Allied air forces.

Inevitably, the DC-3 suffered its share of accidents during its early operations, though none was the fault of the aircraft. The first occurred on 9 February 1937, when DC-3 NC16073 of United Air Lines crashed into San Francisco Bay, killing all eleven on board. An investigation revealed that the co-pilot had accidentally dropped his microphone, which jammed the elevator controls and sent the aircraft into a shallow dive from which there was no time to recover. Three more aircraft were lost in 1937, one a KLM DC-3 in the Dutch East Indies, and four in 1938, but there were no losses in 1939. The cause of the documented losses ranged from icing to collisions with high ground and bad weather. The fact that no DC-3 was ever lost to structural failure stands as a proud testament to the skill and expertise of the aircraft's designers and engineers.

LAPE's DC-2 EC-AGN was requisitioned by the Spanish Republican government.

The DC-2 and DC-3 at War

Although the military derivatives of the DC-2 and DC-3 with their outstanding service during the Second World War do not feature in this narrative, it was inevitable that some aircraft that continued in airline service should be caught up in the conflict. In Spain, the small fleet of five DC-2s operated by LAPE were quickly requisitioned by the Spanish Republican government after the outbreak of the Nationalist uprising in North Africa, which was soon to erupt into civil war.

On 18 July a DC-2 at Tablada, Seville, was ordered to take off with a number of other aircraft, which were to act as makeshift bombers in an attack on rebel forces in Morocco, but it was deliberately damaged by a rebel Spanish officer, who raked it with small-arms fire and made it temporarily unserviceable. All LAPE's DC-2s remained in government hands except for this aircraft, which remained at Tablada; the airfield became the main point of entry for General Francisco Franco's Nationalist forces, which were soon in the process of being ferried by air from Morocco to the Spanish mainland. On 19 and 20 July, Tablada was attacked by Republican Fokker F.VIIs and DC-2s, both types converted to the bombing role by having their small bomb loads dropped through the side doors. In the case of the DC-2s, the attack came so swiftly that it took the defences so completely by surprise that none of the three defending Nieuport 52 fighters had time to take off. The DC-2 at Tablada, once repaired and pressed into service with the Nationalists, was used in a bombing raid on the Republican airfield at Andujar, Andalusia, on the night of 29 July. Further bombing sorties were flown by the Nationalist DC-2 in August, the pilot on each occasion being Captain Carlos Haya, who went on to become Franco's personal pilot before his death in action in February 1938. At that time he was flying a Fiat CR.32 fighter, which collided with a Republican I-15 during a dogfight.

Both Nationalists and Republicans continued to use their DC-2s as bombers until about September 1936, when both sides began to receive purpose-built bombers (from the Germans and Italians in the case of the Nationalists and the Russians and French in the case of the Republicans), whereupon the DC-2s reverted to their transport functions. A primary role was that of VIP transport, with the airliners shuttling to and fro between Spanish and French airfields on various diplomatic missions. These tasks

were always carried out with strong fighter escort. On other missions, French airspace was overflown to avoid the danger of interception; on 17 May 1937, for example, two DC-2s and fifteen I-15s attempted to fly from Lerida, Catalonia, to Bilbao, which was under siege, via the French airfields of Pau and Toulouse. The flight was abandoned because of bad weather in the mountains along the route and the aircraft were impounded by the French authorities.

China

In the Far East, the first to experience enemy action were the DC-2s operated by CNAC, which were operating fast mail and passenger services between some twenty Chinese cities when the Sino-Japanese war erupted in 1937. Although advances by the Imperial Japanese Army denied access to CNAC's former air routes, this proved to be a busy time for the airline, as its aircraft were always filled with diplomats, journalists and official delegations of one kind or another.

The war caught up with CNAC in earnest on 24 August 1938, when a DC-2 named *Kweilin*, bound for Chungking with fourteen passengers on board and piloted by an American, Hugh Woods, was attacked by eight Japanese fighters only a few minutes after leaving Hong Kong. The Japanese machine-gun fire killed nine of his passengers and, with his aircraft badly damaged, Woods dived through cloud and ditched in a river. The Japanese continued to strafe the aircraft as it floated and there were only three survivors, including the pilot. The aircraft was salvaged from the river and repaired, only to be caught in a strafing attack on Chungking just as it

Captain Carlos de Haya, a talented pilot serving with the Spanish Nationalist forces, flew several bombing missions in the sole Nationalist DC-2.

A CNAC DC-2 pictured over Shanghai.

was about to take off for Hong Kong. The aircraft was set on fire and eight of the thirteen passengers were killed, together with the pilot, Walter Kent, who was hit in the back by a 20-mm cannon shell.

CNAC's damaged DC-3, with most of its starboard wing destroyed by a Japanese fighter attack.

The hybrid 'DC Two and a Half' pictured in Hong Kong after its 860-mile flight from Chungking.

The Japanese attacks may not have been deliberate attempts to destroy civil aircraft. CNAC's DC-2s had briefly been commandeered by the Chinese Air Force, which used them as military transports for some months before returning them to the airline, so it is possible that the Japanese pilots assumed they were still in military service.

Hugh Woods, who had so narrowly escaped with his life on the previous occasion, now had another close brush with death when he was again attacked by Japanese fighters, this time while flying a DC-3. He managed to land and evacuate the passengers and crew, but the fighters continued to strafe the aircraft and destroyed its starboard wing. In Hong Kong, William L. Bond, CNAC's manager, was determined to salvage the damaged DC-3: every aircraft was precious. The problem was that there was no spare DC-3 wing in the whole of China. There was, however, a spare DC-2 wing. No one knew whether a DC-3 would fly with a DC-2 wing on one side, but it was decided to try it. The spare wing was duly flown to the stranded aircraft, lashed to the fuselage underside of another DC-2, and fitted to the stub of the DC-3's wing. Then, with Hugh Woods at the controls, the hybrid aircraft made the 860-mile flight back to Hong Kong, and the pilot reported that the asymmetric wings had made hardly any difference to its flying characteristics. That particular machine passed into aviation legend as the one and only 'DC Two and a Half'.

Europe

The outbreak of war on 3 September 1939 made little difference to the Royal Dutch Airline, KLM, which continued to operate its medium-haul European services very much as usual. Then, in the afternoon of 26 September, DC-3 PH-ASM *Mees* (Titmouse), en route from Stockholm to Amsterdam

KLM DC-3 *Roek* in the bright orange paintwork applied to the airline's fleet for identification on the outbreak of war in 1939. (KLM)

with fifteen passengers and five crew and flown by Captain Jan Moll, was attacked by a German fighter, a Swedish passenger being killed. Moll managed to land the aircraft safety, but after that the airline painted its aircraft bright orange overall to avoid further identification problems.

KLM operations continued without further incident until 10 May 1940, when the Germans launched their Blitzkrieg in western Europe. On that day, despite the fact that the country was neutral, Holland was subjected to heavy air attacks and five KLM DC-2s (PH-ALD, PH-AKN, PH-AKO, PH-AKP and PH-AKK) were destroyed on the ground at Schiphol Airport by aircraft from Luftwaffe's KG.4. At this time, a number of other KLM airliners were routed outside the Netherlands; some of these managed to fly to Britain, while others were located at airfields in the Middle East, from where they had been serving the Palestine–Indonesia–Australia routes.

The DC-3s that had escaped to Britain were interned at Shoreham Airport. After negotiations, the British Air Ministry and the Dutch government in exile agreed to use the KLM aircraft and their crews to replace the de Havilland Albatross airliners, with which BOAC had been running a scheduled service between Heston Aerodrome and Lisbon, Portugal, although such flights were restricted to the carriage of diplomats, military personnel, VIPs and persons with government approval.

The UK–Lisbon service operated up to four times per week. From 20 September 1940, passengers were flown from Whitchurch (although Heston continued as the London terminus for KLM from 26 June till 20 September 1940), and for Lisbon, the pre-war grass airfield at Sintra was used until October 1942, when the new runway was ready at Portela Airport, on the outskirts of Lisbon. By June 1943, over

500 KLM/BOAC flights had carried 4,000 passengers.

Originally, five Douglas DC-3s and one Douglas DC-2 airliner were available, but with the loss of a DC-3 on 20 September 1940 in a landing accident at Heston, and the destruction of another DC-3 in November 1940 by Luftwaffe bombing at Whitchurch, only four aircraft remained: DC-2 G-AGBH *Edelvalk* (ex-PH-ALE), DC-3 G-AGBD *Buizerd* (ex-PH-ARB), DC-3 G-AGBE *Zilverreiger* (ex-PH-ARZ), and DC-3 G-AGBB *Ibis* (ex-PH-ALI). In 1939, with war tensions in Europe increasing, KLM had painted their DC-2s and DC-3s bright orange to mark them clearly as civilian aircraft. BOAC repainted the aircraft in camouflage, with British civil markings

A BOAC Douglas DC-3 silhouetted by searchlights against the backdrop of the Rock of Gibraltar, pictured before its departure to London. The Whitchurch–Lisbon route was extended to Gibraltar in 1943.

and red/white/blue stripes like all BOAC aircraft, but without the Union Flag. They were later marked with their Dutch bird names under the cockpit windows. The interiors remained in KLM colours and markings.

The aircraft flying the Lisbon–Whitchurch route were left unmolested after the beginning of the war. Both Allied and Axis powers respected the neutrality of countries such as Portugal, Sweden and Switzerland and refrained from attacking flights into and out of those nations. The war over the Bay of Biscay, which is north of Spain and off the west coast of France, began to heat up in 1942, as the Battle of the Atlantic intensified and U-boats in transit were subjected to increased Allied air attack.

The BOAC aircraft flying the Lisbon–Whitchurch route were now in real danger, as was shown on 15 November 1942 when G-AGBB *Ibis* was attacked by a single Messerschmitt Bf 110 fighter and suffered damage to its port wing, engine nacelle and fuselage. The DC-3 managed to reach Lisbon, where repairs were carried out.

Then, at 7.35 am on 1 June 1943, *Ibis* took off from Lisbon for Whitchurch on what was to be its last flight. Its flight number, 777, was to become known throughout the world. Two hundred miles northwest of the coast of Spain it was attacked by eight Junkers 88G heavy fighters of *Kampfgeschwader* 40 (KG40) operating out of Kerlin and shot down into the sea with the loss of all thirteen passengers and four crew. Among the passengers was Leslie Howard, the celebrated British actor. The destruction of BOAC Flight 777 sparked a controversy that continues to this day, accompanied by many theories about why the aircraft was shot down. One theory was that the Germans believed British Prime Minister Winston Churchill was on board. The idea was dismissed as nonsense by Churchill himself, who mentioned it in Volume IV of his *History of the Second World War (The Hinge of Fate)*:

'The brutality of the Germans was only matched by the stupidity of their agents. It is difficult to understand how anyone could imagine that with all the resources of Great Britain at my disposal I should have booked a passage in an unarmed and unescorted plane from Lisbon and flown home in broad daylight...'

In January 1939 the Belgian airline Sabena took delivery of its first DC-3 (OO-AUH) which arrived by sea in crates to be assembled in Belgium by Fokker. A second aircraft, OO-AUI, arrived later in the month. When Belgium was attacked by Germany on 10 May 1940 both DC-3s managed to escape to Britain, landing at Hendon, where they were attached to No. 24 Squadron RAF for communications duties. On 23 May 1940, OO-AUI was shot down over Merville by German fighters; two members of the crew were killed and others wounded. Later, the other DC-3, OO-AUH, was authorized to fly to Leopoldville in the Belgian Congo with other Sabena airliners which had escaped to Britain, mainly Savoia-Marchetti SM-78s. During a refuelling stop in Algeria all the Belgian aircraft were seized by the Vichy French authorities at Oran and handed over to the Italians.

Germany

The German airline Deutsche Luft Hansa operated at least ten DC-3s during the Second World War, all of them war booty. Five aircraft (PH-ALH, PH-ALV, PH-ASK, PH-ASM and PH-ASR) were seized in

KLM DC-3 *Ibis* was shot down by Ju 88G fighters northwest of the Spanish coast with the loss of all on board. (KLM)

Holland and given the German registrations D-ABUG, D-ARPF, D-AOFS, D-ATJG and D-ABBF. The latter was lost in a landing accident in Madrid on 9 December 1942 and was replaced by D-ATZP, originally a Belgian aircraft (OO-AUH) which had been captured by the Italians in Algiers and passed on to the Germans. D-ATJG was also lost, possibly in an air attack in late 1944. All the other former Dutch machines survived the war.

In contrast, all four Czech DC-3s seized after the German annexation of Czechoslovakia in 1939 were lost during the Second World War. D-AAIE (formerly OK-AIE) was damaged beyond repair in an air attack on Echterdingen in August 1944; D-AAIF (OK-AIF) was destroyed in an attack in 1943; D-AAIH (OK-AIH) crashed on take-off from Berlin/Tempelhof on 29 October 1940; and D-AAIG (OK-AIG) was lost after making an emergency landing off Frederikstad, Norway, on 21 April 1944.

All the above aircraft were requisitioned by the Luftwaffe during the war, and carried military codes.

Japan

In February 1938, Mitsui and Company Ltd, the U.S.-based subsidiary of the parent company in Japan, bought the licence-manufacturing rights to build and sell the DC-3 for $90,000, acquiring all the necessary technical data and being supplied with two unassembled DC-3s (Douglas code numbers 2055 and 2056). Unknown to Douglas, this transaction had taken place at the behest of the Imperial Japanese Navy. In Japan, the two DC-3s were assembled and served as the pattern aircraft for the Nakajima L2D2, which became the IJN's standard transport aircraft. Powered by Mitsubishi Kinsei radial engines and given the code-name Tabby by the Allies, the L2D2 served throughout the Pacific War.

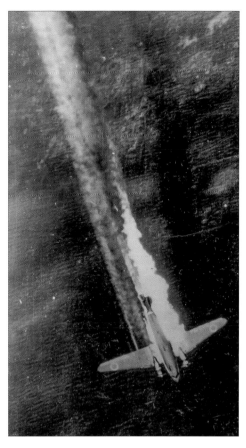

A Japanese L2D2 transport descending in flames over Bono Bay in the Philippines on 21 May 1945.

The United States

Following the Japanese attack on Pearl Harbor in December 1941, many DC-3s serving with the nation's airlines were diverted to military transport contracts, leaving passenger services greatly depleted. For example, six of Delta Air Lines' DC-3s were requisitioned by the military, leaving four aircraft to keep the airline in the passenger business. The same was true across the spectrum of U.S. commercial aviation during the war years, and it was not until large numbers of military C-47s became available for civilian use from 1945 that normality was restored.

The U.S. Navy battleships USS *West Virginia* (BB-48) (sunken at left) and USS *Tennessee* (BB-43) shrouded in smoke following the Japanese air raid on Pearl Harbor. (USN)

The DC-3 in Post-War Years

The tremendous run-down of the Allied air forces in the months after the Second World War resulted in many thousands of war-surplus transport aircraft becoming available for sale to airline operators. Foremost among these was the magnificent Douglas C-47, the military transport version of the DC-3 airliner, known to the RAF and Commonwealth air forces as the Dakota. These aircraft were snapped up in their hundreds by embryo airlines and air freight companies around the world, refurbished and pressed into service. Mostly, the civilian C-47/DC-3 operators continued to refer to their aircraft as Dakotas, abbreviated to 'Daks' in familiar usage.

United States

Post-war, in the United States, the DC-3 was soon rendered obsolete on the main airline routes by more advanced, higher-capacity types such as the Lockheed Constellation and Douglas DC-6, but it continued to serve in large numbers on secondary routes for many more years, operated by numerous air companies.

United Kingdom

For the UK DC-3 operators, an unexpected chance of profit came only three years after the end of the war. On 26 June 1948, Dakotas of No. 46 Group RAF and C-47s of the 60th and 61st Troop Carrier Groups of the USAF began ferrying supplies into Berlin, land access to the city having been cut off by the Russians. These operations marked the start of the Berlin Airlift, the massive airlift operation that was to last a year.

Within a few weeks of the airlift starting, the RAF's Dakota force was augmented by eighteen chartered DC-3s belonging to Air Contractors (G-AIWC, G-AIWD and

N834TP started life as a C-47A-15-DK and served with the USAAF, RAF (as a Dakota III) and the South African Air Force before being converted to a DC-3TP. In its latter years it was based at the U.S. National Test Pilot School at Mojave Airport, California. The turboprop-powered aircraft was written off in a non-fatal accident on 4 February 2009. (Alan Radecki)

Former C-47 Dakota G-AKAY was Sivewright Airways' contribution to the Berlin Airlift. It was sold to Malaysia in 1951. (Air Britain/R.A. Scholefield)

G-AIWE), Air Transport (G-AJVZ), British Nederland Air Services (G-AJAX), BOAC (G-AGIZ, G-AGNG, G-AGNK), Ciros Aviation (G-AIGD, G-AKJN), Hornton Airways (G-AKLL), Kearsley Airways (G-AKAR, G-AKDT), Scottish Airlines (G-AGWS, G-AGZF), Sivewright Airways (G-AGKY), Trent Valley Aviation (G-AJPF) and Westminster Airways (G-AJAY, G-AJAZ).

All the chartered DC-3s were initially based alongside the RAF aircraft at Lübeck, but with congestion at the latter airfield reaching a critical level, on 5 October they were transferred to Fühlsbüttel, the civil airport of Hamburg which was controlled by the Civil Aviation Control Commission of Germany.

The participation of the civilian DC-3s in the airlift did not come about without its set of problems. For one thing, there was no time to send out advance parties to explore what facilities were available in Germany, to obtain a full briefing on operational procedures, radio frequencies, loading arrangements and so on, or to set up a proper maintenance organization. It speaks well for the initiative and resource of the operators that, although the first aircraft only arrived in Germany on 4 August, they were able to commence operations without any delay the next morning. Difficulties had to be overcome, and strenuous efforts had to be made, not only by the operators themselves, but also by the RAF, who showed themselves always ready to give prompt and immediate assistance. As an example, on the eve of the start of the civil operation, despatch riders had to be sent to RAF stations in Germany to obtain radio crystals for the civil aircraft sets, so that they could be tuned to the special radio frequencies in use. Also, the army asked that the civil DC-3s carry the same standard payload of 7,480 lb (3,393 kg) as the RAF's Dakotas. As this weight was in excess of the 6,000 lb (2,722 kg) allowed by the civil aircraft's Certificate of Airworthiness, applications were immediately made to the Air Registration Board for the standard RAF load to be carried, but clearance was not received until 15 August. A further difficulty was that the payloads of individual aircraft varied, as some companies had not fully stripped the interiors of passenger furnishings and other unnecessary dead weight. This problem was also solved by 16 August, when all civilian DC-3s began operating with the 7,480-lb (3,393-kg) payload.

The supply of spare parts, the consumption of which rose steeply with the intensity of flying, was a source of constant anxiety, particularly with the DC-3 companies operating American equipment. Most of these companies were to haunt the civil airlift almost to the very end, to an ever-decreasing degree, but they never loomed as large as they did in the first three months of operations.

DC-3 G-AHCY of British European Airways. This aircraft was also a war surplus C-47A.

For many of these companies, formed in the early post-war years by enthusiastic young men who had survived the war and who had scraped together every penny to purchase surplus transport aircraft, the Berlin Airlift was to be their heyday and also their swansong, for the majority did not last beyond the early 1950s. For those that did survive the DC-3 remained a principal workhorse for many years.

In the United Kingdom, the main DC-3 operator in the mid-1950s was the British European Airways Corporation, which had come into being in August 1946 as a division of BOAC. Using a fleet of DC-3s transferred from BOAC, BEA began operations on its own account with services to Marseille, Rome, Athens, Madrid, Bordeaux, Gibraltar, Lisbon, Amsterdam, Brussels, Paris, Gothenburg, Stockholm, Helsinki, Copenhagen and Oslo. By the beginning of 1947, services had been extended to include Istanbul, Ankara, Hamburg, Berlin, Frankfurt, Vienna and Prague. In March 1955, forty-six DC-3s were still in service with BEA, but they were gradually being replaced by new types such as the turboprop-powered Vickers Viscount and Airspeed Ambassador. BEA named its Dakotas 'Pionairs', eventually disposing of the last example in May 1963.

Other UK DC-3 operators in 1955 were Airmobility, conducting passenger and freight charters with five DC-3s; Air Kruise (Kent) Ltd with four, operating out of Lydd in Kent; BKS Air Transport (five, with bases at Newcastle and Southend); Cambrian Air Services at Cardiff (3); Dan-Air Services at Blackbushe (2); Derby Aviation (2); Eagle Aviation, also at Blackbushe (2); Hunting-Clan at Croydon (4); Manx Airlines (2); Scottish Airlines at Prestwick (1); Starways, which operated scheduled weekly services from Liverpool/Speke to Lourdes with three DC-3s; Skyways Ltd at Stansted (4); Transair Ltd at Croydon, operating eight DC-3s on newspaper and mail deliveries, inclusive tours, passenger and freight charters and a regular scheduled passenger service to Jersey; and Wolverhampton Aviation Ltd (2).

A very large proportion of the DC-3s in service with aviation companies in the post-wart years were in fact converted war-surplus C-47s, and as time went by

HB-IRI was one of the original DC-3s delivered to Swissair in 1937. It was sold to Ozark Airlines, flying as N142D until 1966. (Swissair)

Air France DC-3 F-BAXP seen at Manchester Airport in 1952. Formerly a military C-47A, this was one of the hundreds of C-47s refurbished and converted to civilian use after the war.

One of Swissair's fleet of converted C-47s, HB-IRH was lost in 1957 after it entered a spin and crashed in Lake Constance. (Swissair)

First flown in 1947, Douglas DC-3C OO-AUX was leased from Delta Air Transport by Sabena. It was damaged beyond repair in a taxiing accident at Amsterdam-Schiphol on 9 May 1970. (Tony Hancke)

the name Dakota was almost universally adopted to describe the civilian aircraft.

Europe

The DC-3 found its way into the airlines of most European nations in the post-war years. It was the most important type on the inventory of Swissair; four of the original five aircraft purchased before the war remained in service. Post-war purchases included DC-3D HB-IRB, originally N34973, which was sold to Swissair in 1946. In 1962 it was sold to Norway as lN-LMK, then to the South African company Comair as ZS-DXW, and finally to Ethiopia as ET-AIB. A second DC-3D, HB-IRC, originally NC34982, was also purchased in 1946 and was used by Swissair's Aviation Training School until it was sold to South Africa as ZS-FRJ. It later flew with Swazi-Air as 3D-ABI until its withdrawal in 1976. The other nine aircraft used by Swissair in the 1940s and 1950s were all converted C-47s.

Swissair's post-war DC-3 story followed much the same pattern as that of other DC-3 users, with aircraft purchased from the vast war-surplus stocks, refurbished and converted to civil use, and then sold on to other companies as the original users acquired more modern equipment. KLM, the original European DC-3 operator,

DC-3 ZS-BXF is one of the classic aircraft maintained by the South African Airways Museum at Rand Airport, Germiston. It is still used for scenic pleasure flights. (SAA Museum)

Another South African company, Rovos Air, was established in 2002 at Randpark Ridge and offered nostalgia flights in vintage piston-engined aircraft like ZS-CRV, which was named *Delaney* in honour of a girl born on board during one of its trips. (Rovos Air Archives)

Air India International was a major DC-3 user. This aircraft, VT-CGP, was photographed at London Heathrow in March 1956. The livery is silver, white, red and black. (Air-Britain Archives)

started to rebuild its network in August 1945, immediately after the end of the war with Japan, its initial priority being to re-establish its route to Batavia. Domestic and European services resumed in September 1945, initially using its fleet of DC-3s and some Douglas DC-4 aircraft. In all, including the pre-war purchases, KLM used fifty-one DC-3s, the last examples being retired in 1964.

Civilian DC-3s served in the Berlin Airlift alongside Dakotas of RAF Transport Command, which made extensive use of the type. (Air Atlantique)

Contemporaries and Successors

Among the airliner types that were contemporary with the DC-3, only one came anywhere near the Douglas aircraft in terms of passenger capacity. This was the seventeen-seat Junkers 52/3m. Derived from a single-engined design, it was powered by three 660-hp BMW 132A-1 radial engines, although many other powerplants were installed in the course of its career. Production began in 1932, the first seven examples being delivered to the Brazilian company Lloyd Aero Boliviano. Understandably, the biggest customer was Deutsche Luft Hansa, which had a fleet of eighty before the war, and eventually no fewer than 231 Ju 52/3m aircraft were registered under the airline's flag, although most were operated on behalf of the Luftwaffe during the Second World War. The aircraft soon made a name for itself as one of the most reliable types in service anywhere in the world; DLH stated that emergency landings were reduced from seven per million kilometres to 1.5 after the airliner's introduction. The Ju 52/3m was operated by twenty-eight airlines worldwide. Like the DC-3, the Ju 52/3m is best remembered for its role as a military transport during the Second World War, 2,822 being produced for military purposes between 1939 and 1945. Of these, only 190 were left at the end of the war in Europe.

The closest French contemporary with the DC-3 was the Marcel Bloch MB.220,

The tough and reliable Junkers 52/3m was immensely popular with commercial aviation companies throughout the world. This example was used by the Sino-German Eurasia Aviation Company.

The Bloch MB.220 was a French twin-engine passenger transport aircraft built by Société des Avions Marcel Bloch during the 1930s. After the war, Marcel Bloch changed his name to Marcel Dassault, which had been his name during his time in the French Resistance.

Above: Six Fiat G.18V airliners were delivered to the Avio Linee Italiane (ALI), which operated them on its European routes until the outbreak of war.

Left: Andrei N. Tupolev's ANT-35 was an excellent design, but was handicapped by its limited passenger capacity.

but in terms of numbers it paled into insignificance, with only seventeen built. First flown in December 1935, it was used by Air France on European routes, the first service being flown on 27 March 1938 between Le Bourget and Croydon. Most MB.220s were impressed as military transports by the Free French and Vichy forces, and Air France continued to operate the surviving aircraft on short-range European routes after the war, but they were withdrawn in 1949.

Italy's potential challenger to the DC-3 was the Fiat G.18. A conventional low-wing monoplane, it could seat eighteen passengers and, like the DC-3, its main undercarriage units retracted into the engine nacelles, leaving the wheels partly exposed. Three G.18s entered service with the Avio Linee Italiane (ALI), Fiat's own airline, but they were reported to be underpowered and Fiat produced a revised version, the G.18V, which had more powerful 1,000-hp Fiat A.80 engines, a redesigned fin and a long dorsal strake. Six of these were delivered to ALI, which operated them on its European routes until the outbreak of war. In June 1940, ALI was brought under control of the Regia Aeronautica. and the G.18s were put to use as transports. Among other operations, they flew troops to Albania in November 1940 as part of the campaign against Greece. By the

time of the Italian Armistice in September 1943 only one remained operational, three having been captured by the Germans and another serving with the Italian Fascist Republican forces in northern Italy. This latter aircraft was involved in a major accident on 30 April 1944 when, loaded with munitions, it exploded on the runway at Bresso, north of Milan.

The Soviet Union's answer to the DC-3 was the Tupolev ANT-35, an all-metal, low-wing monoplane powered by two 800-hp Tumansky M-85 engines (licence-produced Gnome-Rhone 14Ks). With provision for ten passengers, it had a retractable undercarriage and first flew in August 1936. In September, during its flight test programme, it flew the 800-mile Moscow–Leningrad–Moscow route in a record time of three hours, thirty-eight minutes, averaging 248 mph.

The prototype was followed by nine production aircraft, designated ANT-35bis and fitted with 1,000-hp Shvetsov M-62IR engines. These entered service with Aeroflot in 1937 and later served as liaison and VIP transport aircraft after 1941. The ANT-35 was manoeuvrable, fast and reliable and was fitted with modern equipment; its main drawback was its uneconomical passenger capacity, which could not be increased. Inevitably, it fell victim to the PS-83 – the Soviet-built DC-3.

Douglas DC-3 Variants

DST: Douglas Sleeper Transport. The initial variant with two 1,000–1,200-hp Wright 1820 Cyclone engines and standard sleeper accommodation for up to sixteen (eight per side) with small upper windows, convertible to carry up to twenty-four day passengers.

DST-A: DST with Pratt & Whitney Twin Wasp engines.

DC-3: Main pre-war production variant fitted with twenty-one passenger seats, powered by two 1,000–1,200-hp Wright R-1820 Cyclone engines

DC-3A: Improved DC-3 with two 1,000–1,200-hp Pratt & Whitney R-1830 Twin Wasp radial piston engines.

DC-3B: Improved DC-3 with two 1,100-hp Wright R-1820-G101 Cyclone or two 1,200-hp Wright R-1820-G202A Cyclone engines.

DC-3C: Designation of 28 additional new aircraft built by Douglas in 1946 for civil airline operation using components from uncompleted USAAF C-117 'Super Dakotas'.

DC-3S: Designation applied to the Super DC-3, an improved DC-3 with a new wing, tail, and two 1,450-hp Pratt & Whitney R-2000-D7 or 1,475-hp Wright R-1820-C9HE Cyclone engines. Only five examples converted by Douglas in 1949/50 from existing DC-3 and R4D airframes.

PS-84: Designation of a 14–28 seat passenger airliner produced in the Soviet Union and powered by two 900-hp Shvetsov M-62 or 1,000-hp Shvetsov Ash-62 engines. With a somewhat smaller span and higher empty weight, it was also equipped with lower-powered engines compared to the DC-3 and the cargo door was transposed to the right-hand side of the fuselage.

C-41A: A single DC-3A (40-070), powered by two 1,200-hp Pratt & Whitney R-1830-21 engines. The Douglas C-41A was used as the personal transport of the U.S. Secretary of State for War. The aircraft was originally a DC-2, modified to DC-3A standard, which had been used for this purpose under the designation C-33.

American service personnel embarking on a Delta Air Lines DC-3, impressed for use as a military passenger transport.
(Delta Air Lines)

Many civilian DC-3s were impressed for military service during the Second World War and were allocated military designations, as follows:

C-48: One DC-3A requisitioned from United Air Lines.

C-48A: Three impressed DC-3As with eighteen-seat interiors.

C-48B: Sixteen former United Air Lines DST-As, impressed into service for use in the air ambulance role, with provision for sixteen stretchers.

C-48C: Sixteen impressed DC-3As with twenty-one-seat interiors.

C-49: The designation allocated to 138 DC-3s impressed by the USAAF after America's entry into the war. Of these, seventy-five were taken from the production lines. The aircraft were given the designations C-49, C-49A, C-49B, C-49C, C-49D, C-49E, C-49F, C-49G, C-49H, C-49J and C-49K depending on their interior configuration, which often differed in minor detail, such as the number of seats installed. Many of the aircraft impressed from airline service were leased back to operate on routes considered to be important by the War Department.

C-50: Fourteen aircraft impressed as personnel transports.

C-51: One aircraft, ordered by Canadian Colonial Airlines and fitted with a door on the starboard side, impressed into service.

C-52: Five DC-3A aircraft, fitted with R-1830 engines, impressed into service.

C-68: Two impressed DC-3As with twenty-one-seat interiors.

C-84: One impressed DC-3B aircraft.

R4D-2: Two Eastern Air Lines DC-3s impressed into USN service as VIP transports, later designated R4D-2F and later R4D-2Z.

R4D-4: Ten impressed DC-3s

R4D-4R: Seven DC-3s impressed as staff transports.

R4D-4Q: Radar countermeasures version of R4D-4.

Mamba-Dakota: One aircraft converted in 1949 for the UK Ministry of Supply as a test-bed, powered by two Armstrong Siddeley Mamba turboprops. This was the first DC-3 to be fitted with turboprop engines.

Airtech DC-3/2000: A DC-3 powered by two PZL ASsz-62IT radial engines, converted by Airtech Canada, Ontario.

Basler BT-67: DC-3 conversion with a stretched fuselage, strengthened structure, modern avionics, and powered by two Pratt & Whitney Canada PT-6A-67R turboprop engines. The aircraft was produced by Basler Turbo Conversions of Oshkosh,

Below: This photograph, taken in 1956, shows the first of three Douglas R4D Skytrain aircraft on the ramp behind the NACA High-Speed Flight Station. Note the designation 'United States NACA' on the side of the aircraft. NACA stood for the National Advisory Committee for Aeronautics, which evolved into the National Aeronautics and Space Administration (NASA) in 1958.

Left: This Basler BT-67 turboprop conversion served with the Guatemalan Air Force. It is seen here at Guatemala City undergoing engine maintenance. (Airplane Pictures)

The Conroy Super-Turbo-Three was a converted Super DC-3 and was powered by a pair of Rolls-Royce Dart turboprops. The Super-Turbo-Three required a 6,000-foot-long runway, limiting its practicality as a commuter airliner. The Super-Turbo-Three ended its days at the Groton Airport, Connecticut. Its cockpit was seriously damaged when it was hit by the wing of a taxiing Trans American Lockheed Hercules on 24 February 1984.

Wisconsin and small numbers were used by civilian and military operators.

BSAS C-47TP Turbo-Dakota: A South African C-47 conversion for the South African Air Force by Braddick Specialized Air Services, with two Pratt & Whitney Canada PT6A-65R turboprop engines, revised systems, stretched fuselage, and modern avionics.

Conroy Turbo-Three: One DC-3 converted by Conroy Aircraft with two Rolls-Royce Dart Mk 510 turboprop engines.

Conroy Super-Turbo-Three: Same as the Turbo-Three but converted from a Super DC-3. One converted.

Conroy Tri-Turbo-Three: Conroy Turbo-Three further modified by the removal of the two Rolls-Royce Dart engines and their replacement by three Pratt & Whitney Canada PT6s (one mounted on each wing and one in the nose).

Greenwich Aircraft Corp Turbo Dakota DC-3: DC-3 conversion with a stretched fuselage, strengthened wing centre section, and updated systems, powered by two Pratt & Whitney Canada PT6A-65AR turboprop engines.

The British Dart Dakotas

Three Dakotas were used by Rolls-Royce in the development of the Dart turboprop engine, which was to power the Vickers Viscount, the first turboprop-powered airliner in the world. Two of them, G-ALXN and G-AMDB, were BEA aircraft, their normal engines being replaced by two RDa 3/2 (505) Darts. A third aircraft, KJ829, was on loan from the RAF. The first machine, G-ALXN, was collected from the Rolls-Royce test establishment at Hucknall in June, 1951, after completion of Rolls-Royce flight trials and issue of the C. of A. Performance tests and crew familiarization preceded a period of regular freight-carrying services by the two aircraft to Hanover, Brussels, Paris, Rome, Stockholm, Copenhagen and Milan.

Two major Dart developments during the Dakota operations were the introduction of the engine and airscrew de-icing system, and of the water/methanol injection system, performed by Rolls-Royce and BEA in close cooperation.

The basic DC-3 design was also used in the evolution of the Douglas B-18 (DB-1), a medium/heavy bomber that won the 1936 USAAC bomber competition. An initial order was placed for 177 machines but only 133 were delivered, the remainder of the order being transferred to the improved

One of the Dart Dakotas used to test the Rolls-Royce Dart turboprop at Hucknall, bearing the test registration G-37-2. (Air-Britain/Mike Dowsing)

B-18A, 217 examples of which were produced. Twenty aircraft were transferred to the Royal Canadian Air Force, in whose service the type was known as the Digby I. In 1939/40, 122 B-18As were converted to B-18B standard by the installation of specialist radio equipment for maritime patrol duties, two aircraft being transferred to the Brazilian Air Force. The B-18 ended its career as a paratroop trainer.

Below: Among the many configurations applied to the DC-3 was a floatplane conversion. This example was pictured at a fly-in at Greenville, Maine, in 2002. (Doug Ronan Aircraft)

Above: The basic DC-3 design was adapted for use as the Douglas DB-1 bomber, of which 133 were delivered to the U.S. Army Air Corps. It was followed by 217 examples of the improved B-18A, three of which are seen here over Hawaii.

The Super DC-3

By the late 1940s, although hundreds of DC-3s continued to render viable service across the world, it was becoming increasingly clear that the type could not go on forever. For one thing, it was not compatible with new transport category requirements that had come into force in the U.S. Rather than replacing the existing DC-3 with an entirely new Douglas-designed aircraft of similar configuration, Douglas decided that the simplest solution would be to carry out major modifications to the existing DC-3 airframe, producing what in effect would be a new aircraft – in other words, a Super DC-3. Under the direction of Douglas Chief Engineer Malcolm K. Oleson, the Douglas engineering team took a standard DC-3 airframe and stretched the fuselage, adding 39 inches to the nose section and 40 inches to the rear cabin, creating an extra 6 feet and 7 inches of usable space. They increased the vertical and horizontal tail surfaces in span and area, and replaced the power plants with the same 1,450-hp Pratt & Whitney R-2000 Twin Wasp engines used in the Douglas DC-4. Shorter, jet ejection-type exhaust stacks increased the usable horsepower. The engine nacelles were

enlarged, wheel well doors were fitted, and a partially retractable tail wheel installed. Smaller outer wing panels were fitted, swept back four degrees at the trailing edge to accommodate the rearward shift in the centre of gravity. Flush rivets and low drag antennas decreased the drag. These changes allowed them to increase the seating capacity to thirty-eight.

The first flight of the Super DC-3 took place on 23 June 1949. The aircraft was designated DC-3S, code number 43158. It showed a top speed to 250 mph and had a service ceiling of 25,000 feet. The USAF showed an interest and evaluated the aircraft as the YC-47F, but opted for

The Super DC-3 was not a commercial success, but 100 aircraft were produced for the U.S. Navy as the R4D-8. Some were later acquired by commercial companies, such as this one in the livery of TransNorthern, seen landing at Anchorage, Alaska, in 2011. (TransNorthern Aviation)

the new Convair C-131 instead. The U.S. Navy, however, contracted with Douglas to convert 100 of their R48-8 variant of the DC-3 to Super DC-3 standard, which kept the project alive for a time, but the aircraft was not a success commercially and only five were built. Three of these were taken up by Capital Airlines, which introduced the first one on the Washington–Atlanta run in July 1950. The other two were retained by Douglas, who fitted one with Rolls-Royce Dart turboprops at the request of Pilgrim Airlines, but it never went into service.

The Would-be DC-3 Replacements

In the immediate post-war years, two American aircraft manufacturers entered the running to produce a viable DC-3 replacement. The first was the Glenn L. Martin Company, which built the Model 2-0-2. Two flying prototypes were produced, the first flying on 22 November 1946; in August 1947 the type became the first twin-engine airliner of U.S. post-war design to receive a CAA type operating certificate. Twenty-five 2-0-2s were completed for Northwest Orient Airlines, plus four for LAN-Chile and two for LAV of Venezuela, LAN-Chile being the first to put the type

into service, in October 1947. Powered by two 2,400-hp R-2800-CA18 engines, the 2-0-2 seated 36–40 passengers in an unpressurized fuselage. Its career came to a halt in 1948, following the crash of a Northwest Airlines 2-0-2 due to structural failure. No further 2-0-2s were built, but Glenn Martin developed an improved version, the 4-0-4, which first flew on 21 October 1950. Between the autumn of 1951 and the spring of 1953 101 Martin 4-0-4s were delivered to Eastern Air Lines (60) and TWA (41).

Two more were delivered to the U.S. Coast Guard as RM-1s. Atlanta-based Southern Airways operated a fleet of twenty-five 4-0-4s; this airline was founded in 1943 but had to wait until the war's end before operating its first passenger service, in June 1949. It began operations with DC-3s and retained these aircraft until the late 1950s, when it re-equipped with 4-0-4s, many of them former Eastern Air Lines aircraft. Unlike most other airlines of the era, Southern never made the move to turboprops and retained its Martin airliners well into the 1970s.

The other manufacturer was Convair, whose Model 240 first flew at San Diego on

Martin 4-0-4 N40422 of Pacific Airlines, which purchased eight aircraft from TWA in 1960 and two more from Eastern in 1962. The aircraft were used on the short-haul San Joaquin Valley route from Los Angeles to San Jose and Oakland. This aircraft was sold to charter company Fiesta Air as N302FA in 1971 and then to Kodiak Western Alaska Airlines in 1976. It was withdrawn from use in the late 1970s.
(Pacific Air Lines)

A restored Convair 240 in the livery of Western Air Lines pictured at the Planes of Fame Air Museum in Arizona, 2005.
(Planes of Fame Museum)

DC-3 SE-CFP in vintage Scandinavian Airlines livery and owned by Flygande Veterane, pictured flying over Lindingö, Sweden, in 1989. Originally a C-47, the aircraft took part in the D-Day operations on 6 June 1944, dropping paratroops of the 101st Airborne Division's 'Easy' Company, the unit that featured in the TV series *Band of Brothers*. (Air Atlantique)

16 March 1947. Also powered by R-2800-CA18 engines, it seated up to forty passengers and immediately met with a favourable reaction from the airlines. By mid-1940 over 150 Convair 240s had been ordered, the largest order coming from American Airlines, which purchased 75 aircraft and introduced the type into scheduled service on 1 June 1948. The basic soundness of the Convair 240 led to a stretched version, the Convair 340, which seated 44 passengers and flew in October 1951. Two hundred and nine Convair 340s were used by several airlines, and were followed by yet another version, the Convair 440 Metroplitan, which appeared in October 1955 and which seated up to 52 passengers. Over 520 Convair 440s were produced, 340 being conversions of the Convair 340 and 86 being new aircraft built to Metropolitan standard.

Douglas Dakota DC-3 (G-ANAF) of the Air Atlantique Historic Flight at Hullavington Airfield, Wiltshire, England, taking off. The aircraft was operated by Air Atlantique on behalf of the Thales Group for development of the Nimrod Mk 3 radar. The radome under the cockpit contained a rotating parabolic antenna. A new pitot tube was fitted to the nose as the original tube under the nose would have interfered with the radar. The APU behind the starboard wing provided electrical power for the radar systems. Note the added vertical stabilizer behind the tail wheel. The aircraft was built in 1944 and apparently participated in the Berlin Airlift. (Adrian Pingstone, Public Domain)

Although the Convair series of twin-engine airliners enjoyed great success, it was an aircraft of foreign design that came closest to providing a true DC-3 replacement. This was the Fokker F27 Friendship, which became one of the most successful European airliners of its time. The F27 was developed during the early 1950s with the expressed intent of producing a capable successor to earlier twin-engine types such as the prolific DC-3. A key innovation was the choice of the well-proven Rolls-Royce Dart turboprop engine, which produced substantially less vibration and noise that provided improved conditions for passengers; another major comfort feature was cabin pressurization. Innovative manufacturing techniques were also employed in the aircraft's construction. The F27 flew for the first time on 24 November 1955 and the first production aircraft was delivered to the Irish airline Aer Lingus in November 1958. By the end of the production run for the Fokker F27 in 1987, a total of 592 units had been completed by Fokker, with another 207 F-27s and FH-227s produced in the U.S. by Fairchild.

Fly on Forever

Such was the proliferation of the Dakota in the decades since the Second World War, serving aviation companies large and small in a host of diverse roles that include aerial spraying, freight transport, passenger service, military transport, missionary flying, parachuting and tourism, that it is impossible to produce a comprehensive list of the companies that still use the aircraft. It is even less feasible to estimate the number of Dakotas still flying in the first quarter of the twenty-first century, although the total certainly adds up to several hundred. In recent times, some company names leap out from the pages of the Dakota story: they include Buffalo Airways of Yellowknife, in Canada's Northwest Territories, whose miscellany of aircraft types included half a dozen Dakotas. In Britain, Coventry-based company Air Atlantique acquired twelve Dakotas; among other duties, they were assigned to the Department of Transport's Maritime Control and Pollution Unit, tasked with spraying dispersant chemicals on oil spills such as that resulting from the grounding of the supertanker MV *Sea Empress* off Milford Haven harbour in southwest Wales in February 1996.

Its large cargo door betraying its C-47B origins, G-AMSV was used by the RAF as a Dakota Mk IV before serving with several aviation companies, eventually becoming one of the Air Atlantique fleet. (Air Atlantique)

Air Atlantique was not quite the end of G-AMSV's story. She is now part of the Indian Air Force's Vintage Flight as VP905 and is seen here awaiting the installation of engines during the final stages of restoration. (Indian Air Force)

Buffalo Airways Dakotas at Yellowknife, Northwest Territories. While Buffalo Airways hauls cargo to remote destinations, the airport is also home to several passenger services. (Buffalo Airways)

To the delight of enthusiasts, gatherings of Dakotas still take place around the world. These three aircraft, in line astern, assembled at Duxford in 2014 to mark the 70th anniversary of D-Day. Leading the line is 2100884 / L4-D' (N147DC) c/n 19347, operated by Aces High and based at Dunsfold. Next comes 2100882 / 3X-P (N473DC) c/n 19345, based at East Kirkby. Built in 1944 as 42-100882, she was transferred to the RAF as TS422 and later flew with the RCAF with the same serial. Retired in 1966, she now flies in the markings of the 87th Troop Carrier Squadron, a unit that flew in both D-Day and Market Garden operations. She is based at the Lincolnshire Aviation Heritage Centre, East Kirkby, UK. The third aircraft is 224064 / ID-N (N74589) c/n 9926, based at Waterbury Oxford Airport, Southbury, Connecticut. (Cas K. Jackson Photography)

One of the best-loved Dakotas on the airshow circuit is 'Whiskey 7', owned by the National Warplane Museum in Geneseo, New York. U.S. The aircraft was the lead ship of the 37th Troop Carrier Squadron, dropping elements of the 82nd Airborne Division near Sainte-Mère-Eglise, France, in the early hours of 6 June 1944. (Cas K. Jackson Photography)

Among the many tasks performed by the DC-3 and its turboprop conversions is fire fighting. Here, a Basler Turboprop variant is seen dropping fire-retardant material from an under-fuselage hopper. (Basler Turboprops)

Ever since aircraft were used in support of scientific expeditions to the Antarctic, the DC-3 and its turboprop conversions have played a leading role. Pictured in March 1960 at Naval Air Facility McMurdo Sound (now known as McMurdo Station), this U.S. Navy R4D-8 operated as part of the U.S. Antarctic Research Programme. Note the legend *Wilshie Duit* (Will she do it) on the nose. (U.S. Navy)

For many decades, the Royal Australian Air Force Antarctic Flight assisted the Australian National Antarctic Research Expeditions (ANARE) to explore, map and survey using a variety of fixed-wing aircraft. Here, a Dakota is being hauled ashore at Mawson in 1960, having been shipped by sea with outer wings removed. (RAAF)

Basler turboprop conversion C-GVKB operated by Kenn Borek Air Ltd in the Antarctic wastes. (Kenn Borek Air)

Left and below: Turboprop-powered Dakotas of Kenn Borek fitted with skis. A Canadian company based at Calgary, Alberta, Kenn Borek Air has a fleet of nine Basler BT-67 aircraft and has been operating in Antarctica since 1985. (Kenn Borek Air)

A DC-3 Pilot's Story

**Simon Lannoy,
DC3 pilot for Intra Airways flying from
Jersey on European routes.**

I completed my Commercial Pilot's Licence at Oxford and my first job in Jersey was with Bayley Air Charter in 1972 flying an Aztec, single pilot. Typically I flew Cork to Spain and other European routes, passengers or freight. We had no dinghies and no fire extinguishers. If we were flying lobsters we had to fly below 7,000 feet direct across the Bay of Biscay, otherwise they would degrade and die.

I applied to Intra Airways in March 1973. At the time they were operating three DC-3s on the British Register. They were G-AKNB, MPY and MYJ. My first impression of a DC-3 was that it was huge and impressive. The cockpit, high off the ground, and its two big props turned by the Pratt & Whitney Twin Wasp R1830 engines are enormous. It was my dream job, flying an old Dak from Jersey.

People used to talk about the unfortunate characteristic of a tailwheel aeroplane and the gyroscopic effect when the tail came up. They had developed this mythical reputation of being cantankerous but as I was to find out, it's what you get used to. This was going to be my first tailwheel experience, no introduction on a chipmunk or other smaller tailwheel, straight to the DC-3.

I was in my 20s so it didn't faze me. My first encounter with the aircraft was on the ramp at Jersey – no ground school. I was just given a set of BEA technical notes on the type. My first recollection is getting in and struggling up the steep floor holding onto the seats and making my way up to the cockpit. At that stage we operated with two pilots and one cabin crew.

The main tasks of the external walk-around were to make sure the control locks were out on the ailerons, the undercarriage pins were out, the pitot tube cover was removed, to check the condition of the tyres and to have a general look at the fuselage and control surfaces. However, the external check was mainly to look for hydraulic leaks which was something you needed to be aware off. The ground crew would pull the props through at least three revolutions per engine to be prevent a hydraulic lock. Some of the captains would open the small crew door and jump onto one of the blades to exit the aircraft! The DC-3s were always parked on the ramp in a suitable direction to start the engines and taxi off, no push back.

INTRA AIRWAYS 1973

On that first day you would have thought my role, as the first officer, would be to observe, but it was straight in and hands on. Sitting in the right-hand leather seat, the harness was of the Sutton type, and once ensconced there was plenty of room – even a nice sliding widow for direct vision. All the controls fell to hand apart from the undercarriage levers which were a nightmare next to the captain's seat. Its operation often led to skinned knuckles – sometimes we would wear gloves.

There was no cockpit pre-flight check list as such, it was all done from memory with a look around the cockpit to make sure everything was set for engine start.

GRAND TOTAL 1251·45

Year 1973		AIRCRAFT		Captain	Holder's Operating Capacity	Journey or Nature of Flight		DAY FLYING			NIGHT FLYING			Instrument Flying	REMARKS
Month	Date	Type	Markings			From	To	In Charge	Second P2	Dual P3	In Charge	Second P2	Dual P3		
—	—	—	—	—	—	— Totals brought forward		1046·10		153·15	47·00			5·20 222·50	
MARCH	16	DC3	MYJ	STUART	P.3	JERSEY – JERSEY				1·35				P.H./W.L SOAR/N 12.13	
"	16	DC3	MYJ	STUART	P.1	JERSEY – JERSEY		1·00						P.H./W.L FAMIL. 12.13	TRG
"	19	DC3	MYJ	STUART	P1	JERSEY – JERSEY		2·00						P.H./W.L 12.13	TRG
"	19	DC3	MYJ	STUART	P1	JERSEY – JERSEY		2·00						P.H./W.L 12.13	TRG
"	20	DC3	MYJ	STUART	P1	JERSEY – JERSEY		1·30						P.H./W.L 12.13. Single engine TRG	
"	20	DC3	MYJ	SMART	P1	JERSEY – DINARD		·30						P.H./W.L Cross Country TRG.	
"	20	DC3	MYJ	STUART	P1	DINARD – JERSEY		·30						P.H./W.L Cross Country TRG.	
"	21	DC3	MYJ	STUART	P1	JERSEY – JERSEY		1·00						P.H./W.L Single engine c/s +EFATO	
"	24	DC3	KNB	GARDNER	P.3	JERSEY – GUERNSEY			·20						SUPER/N.
"	24	DC3	KNB	GARDNER	P.3	GUERNSEY – JERSEY			·20						SUPER/N
"	24	DC3	KNB	GARDNER	P.3	JERSEY – SOUTHEND			1·25						SUPER/N
"	24	DC3	KNB	GARDNER	P3	SOUTHEND – GSY			1·35					·15	SUPER/N.
"	24	DC3	KNB	GARDNER	P3	GSY – JERSEG			·20					·20	SUPER/N.
"	30	DC3	MYJ	STUART	P.1	JERSEY – JERSEY		·30						P.H./W.L 12.13 TRG.	
"	30	DC3	MYJ	STUART	P1	JERSEY – JERSEY						1·20			P.H./W.L 1199	
APRIL	5	DC3	MYJ	STUART	P.1	JERSEY – JERSEY		1·00						1·00	BASE CHECK.
"	5	DC3	MYJ	STUART	P1	JERSEY – JERSEY		1·10						1·10	INST. RATING RENEWAL.
"	8	DC3	MPY	STUART	P2	EXETER – JERSEY			1·00						Cross Country
"	8	DC3	MYJ	STUART	P2	JERSEY – DINARD			·30						Cross Country
"	8	DC3	MYJ	STUART	P2	DINARD – JERSEY			·25						Cross Country
"	8	DC3	MYJ	STUART	P2	JERSEY – DINARD			·25						Cross Country
"	8	DC3	MYJ	STUART	P2	DINARD – JERSEY							·30		Cross Country
"	8	DC3	MPY	STUART	P2	JERSEY – DINARD			·25						Cross Country
"	8	DB	MPY	STUART	P2	DINARD – JERSEY			·25						Cross Country
						Totals carried forward		1057·20	3·10	158·30	48·20	·30	5·50	225·00	GRAND TOTAL 1273·00

Two of the aircraft had electric fuel pumps. G-AKNB didn't have them so we had to use a wobble pump, one for each engine. In this case the captain would turn on the magnetos and fuel cocks. The first officer's job was to operate the wobble pump behind the P1 seat, a mechanical fuel pump, just to prime the system and operate the hydraulic pump as the undercarriage and flaps were hydraulic. The Dakota had four fuel tanks carrying over 400 U.S. gallons a side and the fuel tank selector had five positions to access all the tanks.

So we would set the engine controls as throttles one-quarter inch open, mixture to idle cut-off, propellers fully forward to max RPM, air intake cold, gills on the radiator open and oil cooler closed as you wanted the oil to heat up quicker. On the overhead panel were two switches which the captain operated: one was an energize switch, and after energizing he held down the mesh switch too, holding both down. That would start the prop turning. On the sound of the first pop or bang, the first officer would throw in the mixture lever to get it all going by moving the mixture to 'auto rich' position. A frequent cry on the radio would often be that the engines wouldn't mesh. It could be quite a temperamental aircraft to get going. The noise levels were high with the props running just outside the window.

We would constantly be checking for fire and any other problems while waiting for the oil pressure and temperature to warm up. We had to be particularly mindful of the cylinder head temperatures before take-off and thoroughly warm the engines to prevent excessive wear and tear. At the time a number of engine failures had occurred on take-off through abuse and not being warm enough. We would then switch on radios, check everything was ready for taxi and the ground crew would show that the rudder and elevator lock and chocks were removed. We did have a load sheet but

Year 1973		AIRCRAFT		Captain	Holder's Operating Capacity	Journey or Nature of Flight	
Month	Date	Type	Markings			From	To
—	—	—	—	—	—	— Totals brought forward	
October	18	DC3	KNB	Gardner	P1 US	Jersey – Dinard	
"	18	DC3	KNB	Gardner	P2	Dinard – Exeter	
"	18	DC3	KNB	Gardner	P1 US	Exeter – Hurn.	
"	18	DC3	KNB	Gardner	P2	Hurn – Jersey	
"	19	DC3	KNB	Gardner	P1 US	Jersey – Hurn.	
"	19	DC3	KNB	Stanley	P2	Hurn – Jersey	
"	19	DC3	MPZ	Stuart	P2	Jersey – Dinard	
"	19	DC3	MPZ	Stuart	P3	Dinard – Jersey	

we didn't do much with regards to weight and balance; it was done for us.

After a call for radio clearance to Jersey tower the captain, or handing pilot, would taxi out and we would switch to auto pilot which locked the control surfaces and meant we would steer by use of differential breaking. A slow taxi meant you didn't need differential power at all apart from in extreme situations and the tailwheel was fully castoring. It was an easy aircraft to taxi. Very little emergency briefing was carried out at this time.

Power and magneto checks were carried out at the 'hold into wind'; this occurred once the oil was above 40°C and the cylinder head temperature was at 120°C. We would then test each engine separately looking for mag drops, correct cylinder head temperatures, oil temperatures and pressures. We would check the operation of the constant speed propeller too. Then we'd move on to pre-take-off checks, this included the hydraulic system, flaps up, selector neutral, parking brake off, check of controls full and free, trim neutral, mixture to auto rich, air intake cold, propeller speed control fully forward, fuel check contents and selectors, gills, oil cooler and generators. After that the auto pilot would be taken reversed and the tailwheel would be locked once it was lined up (having received clearance for departure by the tower).

You had to be on the ball with any cross-wind take-offs, the power levers would be advanced and the noise was phenomenal. One would hold the wheel into any cross wind, gently pushing forward on the controls to get the tail up (once there was sufficient airflow over the tail feathers) and not too fast. As the tail rose the fun could start as the gyroscopic effect took hold. I remember one particular flight, in a stonking cross wind with a very experienced wartime Halifax pilot, that after the tail had come up the aircraft decided it wanted to be back at the parking spot we had just taxied out off. The aircraft departed the runway skidding across the grass while the captain wrestled with the controls. He brought the DC-3 to a halt by the hangar we had just left and reached into his pocket for a cigarette. We would start the climb when the safety speed of 110 mph was achieved. Once airborne, dab the breaks to stop the wheels spinning and then the non-handling pilot would pull the undercarriage up and raise the flaps, if used.

Gaining altitude, we'd set the climb power and adjust the pitch, climbing at 125 mph. During the climbs and the cruise, if the weather was inclement, rain would pour through the magneto switches and condensation was rife on the windscreens. Along the bottom of the windscreens were gutters to collect the condensation which were supposed to run to outside. Smokers would use these as ashtrays, blocking the vents so the water wouldn't run out. You would often get covered in nicotine-stained brown water.

Although it was a fairly reliable aircraft, single-engine performance, when loaded, was negligible and I did witness an engine failure on take-off which was quite dramatic.

It was quite a light aeroplane to fly. The auto pilot was just a wing leveller and navigation at that stage was basic VOR and NDB. Because they were not pressurized, the cabins would fill up with smoke and there was no air recirculation or filter. We would open the DV windows which meant the smoke from the rear cabin would make its way to the front and go out the windows next to me. Coming back on a flight from Staverton one Sunday afternoon (3 August 1973), I was munching on some sandwiches I had picked up as we had no inflight catering. I didn't finish them and threw the bag with the remaining sandwich out of the window over the sea; next thing I know the radios failed as the bag had gone down the radio cooling scoop behind the cockpit. Lesson learned.

We would come into land using a 3-degree glide slope; we did have an ILS for poor weather and NDB. Speed would be reduced to 90–95 mph, then pitch levers fully fine and throttles set, flaps one stage. The limiting speed on flaps was 125 mph. The undercarriage would be put down at 1,500 feet (and speeds less than 160 mph) and then onward to full flap adjusting for glide slope.

The checks for landing went along the lines of: gills closed, oil coiler closed, check hydraulic pressure, undercarriage down and positive lock, tail wheel locked, mixture auto rich, prop fully forward, allowing for cross wind using a crab to land then touch down on one wheel. No three pointer, just pin on the main wheels and fly it till she ran out of elevator authority, then wheel fully back and keep her straight, remembering that it's not over until it's parked. Raise flaps and open the gill flaps for cooling. For manoeuvring we would then need to unlock the tail wheel and put the auto pilot back in. Once parked at the ramp, the steps were brought up for the passengers to disembark. Shutting down meant idling the engines to allow temperatures to stabilize to 205°C. Then throttles closed, close the mixture levers to idle cut-off and the big props would slow to a halt. Silence.

I completed over 500 hours on the type and looking back I have very fond memories of the aircraft. You could have some fun back then: we had an Elsan toilet in the tail of the aircraft and if the captain went back to use the facilities you could apply the rudder to slosh around the contents while he was in residence.

We were parked waiting to take passengers while another was loading passengers on the other side of the apron. In the left-hand side of the cargo doors was an emergency release lever. One of the

passengers reached up and grabbed the handle by mistake and the door fell out! It was no small door. I am surprised anyone still wanted to fly after that. Because the aircraft was unpressurized many passengers endured unpleasant problems with their ears due to pressure changes. Our normal cruises would be below 10,000 feet but as we climbed or descended this was often still a problem. We had rubber boots for de-icing on the leading edge of the wing and on the horizontal stabilizer which were pneumatic. We also had propeller de-icing fluid but as we were mainly low level we didn't experience much ice, only occasional and it was not a problem.

At some airfields we were allowed to pick up the duty-free allowance for every passenger if they were not using it. This often led to a very large amount of spirits and cigarettes being stored up on the flight deck. No one thought about safety, and getting out in an emergency would have been a nightmare. The only way out was to use the small crew door on to the port engine side.

The weather into Jersey was regularly against us and we could often come back and find that the cloud across the island would be down to 200 feet or less. This meant that we would need to divert to Dinard in France which could lead to an overnight stop – and of course a night in the bar. Talking of bars, one day I flew a DC-3 back from Morlaix single handed. The captain had to spend the entire trip in the Elsan due to his night-time excess.

We did occasionally take the seats out and would fly freight; an example of this was to take a former Air France DC-3 night freighter engine, which we picked up in Dinard, to Exeter to have the engine rebuilt.

Intra had very little business acumen and went around collecting routes that no one wanted. The advantage was that on one occasion when I was coming back from Deauville, another DC-3 was coming back from Caen, and we ended up in formation at low level along the Normandy beaches as we had no passengers on board. Such memories of a great aircraft.

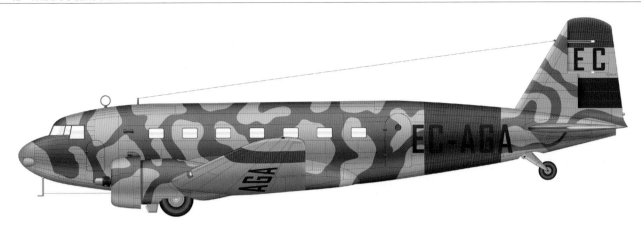

During the Spanish Civil War, the small fleet of five DC-2s operated by the Spanish airline LAPE were quickly requisitioned by the Spanish Republican government after the outbreak of the Nationalist uprising in North Africa, which was soon to erupt into civil war. This camouflaged DC-2, EC-AGA, landed at Ta Qali, Malta, on 12 November 1938, carrying Spanish Republican Minister Bernardo Giner de los Rios and three generals en route to Ankara for the state funeral of Turkish President Mustafa Kemal Atatürk.

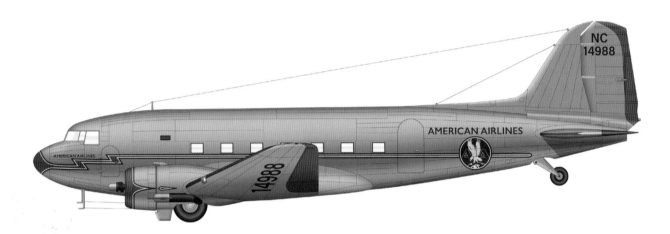

American Airlines' Douglas Sleeper Transport was the first commercial DC-3 and bore the name *Flagship Texas*. It first flew on 17 December, 1935, a date that coincided with the 32nd anniversary of the Wright Brothers' first powered flight at Kitty Hawk. Production of the DST ended in 1941.

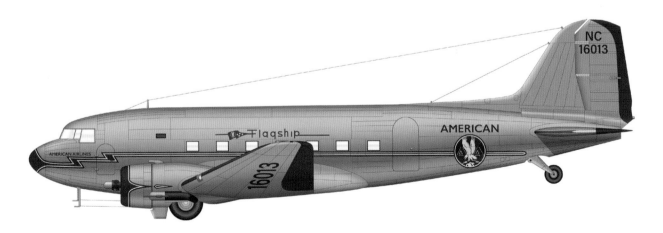

American Airlines' DC-3 NC16013 *Flagship Virginia* was the thirteenth DC-3 to be built and was fitted with a right-hand passenger door. It operated with AA from September 1936 until May 1949, when it was registered XA-HOT and sold to Mexico.

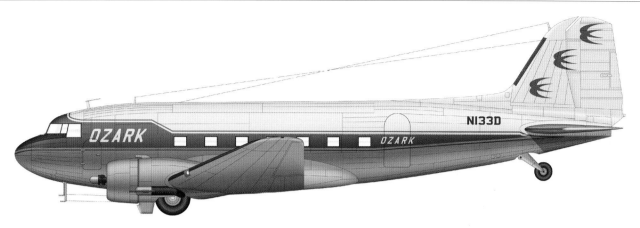

DC-3 N133D of Ozark Air Lines was originally built as a Douglas Sleeper Transport for American Airlines in 1936 and was the sixth aircraft produced. By January 1966 it had logged 60,591 flying hours. In May 1970 it was purchased by Airline Aviation Academy. It was damaged in a landing accident in January 1979, at which point it was the oldest DC-3 still flying. In 2017 it was to be seen minus engines and other parts at Punta Gorda-shell Creek Air Park, Florida.

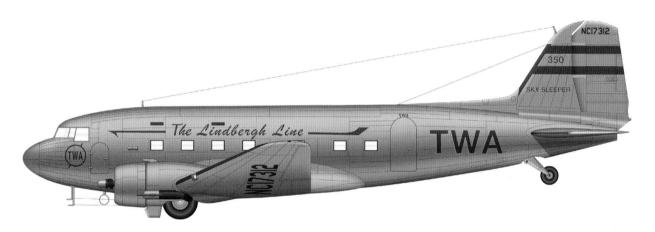

Transcontinental and Western Airlines (TWA) DC-3 *Skysleeper* NC17312 was one of thirty-one aircraft originally ordered by the airline and was the fourth to be delivered.

On 11 April 1936, following the purchase of a single DC-2 for evaluation in 1935, the Soviet government placed an order for eighteen DC-3s (later increased to twenty-one) for operation by the Soviet state airline, Aeroflot. The aircraft was known as the PS-84 in Aeroflot service and received the military designation Lisunov Li-2 after Boris Pavlovich Lisonov, the engineer in charge of the construction programme.

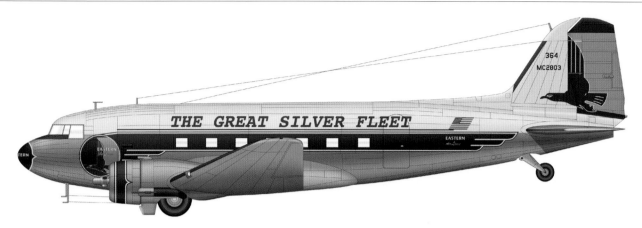

Douglas DC-3 of Eastern Airlines' Great Silver Fleet, seen in 1939. Under the direction of First World War air ace Eddie Rickenbacker, Eastern enjoyed a period of growth and innovation and for a time was the most profitable airline in the post-war era, never needing state subsidy. In the late 1950s, however, Eastern's position was eroded by subsidies to rival airlines and the arrival of the jet age.

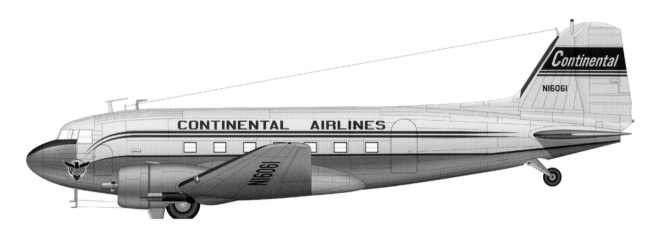

DC-3 N16061 served with United Air Lines from December 1936 to 1953 and carried the name *Mainliner des Moines*. In September 1956 it was purchased by Continental Airlines, which served thirty-five domestic U.S. airports. The aircraft is seen here serving with Continental in 1962.

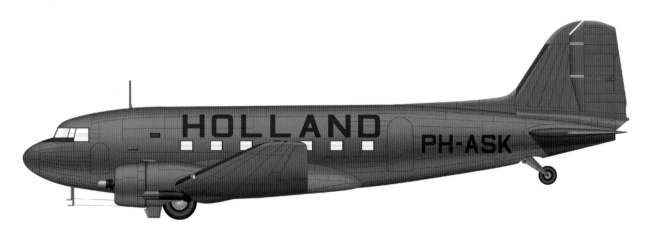

DC-3 PH-ASK of KLM seen in the bright orange paintwork applied after the outbreak of the Second World War for identification after one of their airliners was attacked by a German fighter in September 1939, while Holland was still neutral. After the German invasion, PH-ASK was one of five DC-3s seized as war booty and given the German registration D-AOFS.

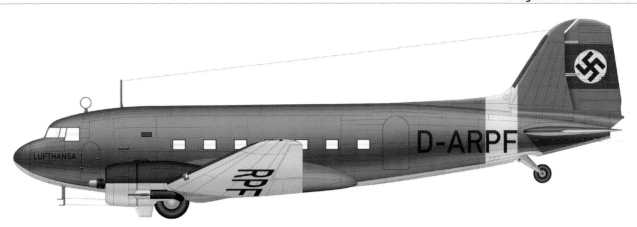

D-ARPF was one of the former KLM DC-3s (PH-ALV) seized by the Germans at Amsterdam-Schiphol Airport. One of the ex-KLM aircraft, DABBF, was lost in a landing accident at Madrid in December 1942 and another, D-ATJG, was destroyed in an air attack in late 1944; all the other former Dutch machines survived the war.

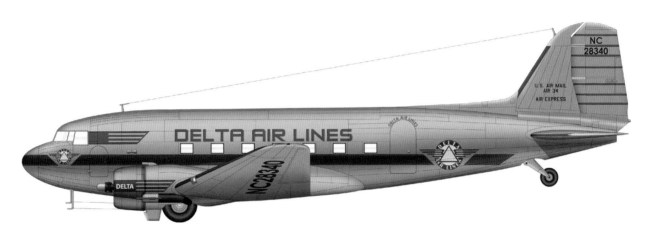

DC-3 NC28340 was delivered brand new to Delta Airlines in November 1940, and flew with them until April 1953, when it was sold to Mohawk. It was extensively damaged in a non-fatal accident in September 1941 after its port landing gear jammed, but was returned to service after repair.

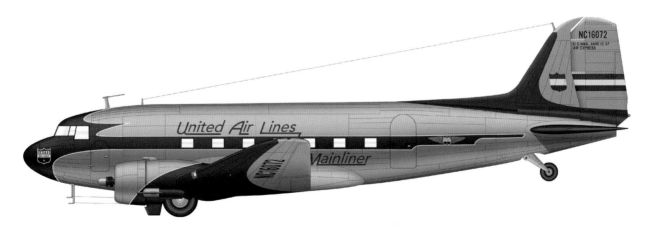

DC-3 NC16072 *State of California* of United Air Lines was destroyed in a hangar fire at Salt Lake City Municipal Airport on 12 January 1941, together with a Western Air Express Boeing 247.

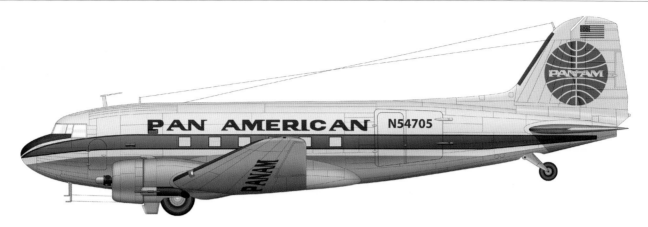

This aircraft was built in 1942 as a C-47A-DK Skytrain and was used as a flying laboratory for experimental equipment before being handed over to the USAAF in March 1944. In March 1946 the aircraft was sold as surplus to Pan American Airways and allocated the registration N54705. It was used mainly on South American routes until June 1960 when it was sold to the Spanish company Spantax SA. It was last seen as a derelict at Alicante.

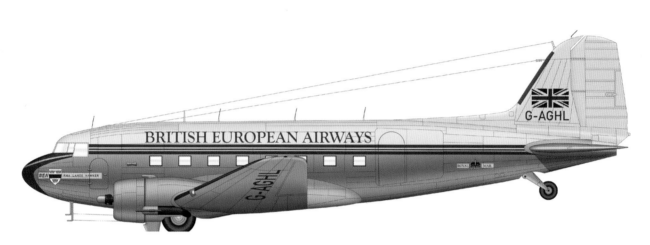

G-AGHL was a former Dakota Mk III and was acquired by British European Airways from surplus RAF stocks in 1946. It bore the name *Lanoe Hawker* after the British First World War air ace Major Lanoe Hawker VC. Note the air-stair passenger door which was fitted as standard to BEA's Pioneer class Dakotas by Scottish Aviation. G-AGHL served BEA from August 1946 until April 1960, when it was sold to Ghana Airways as 9G-AAF.

Built in 1943, G-AMSF was allocated to the RAF as a Dakota Mk IV and after conversion served with BKS Air Charter before passing into private ownership with Don Everall Aviation. On 5 March 1960 it was written off in a non-fatal accident at Birmingham Airport when the No. 2 engine failed immediately after take-off. The Dakota banked to the right, causing the wingtip to strike the ground. The aircraft then cartwheeled and came to rest with a small fire erupting in the area of the No. 1 engine.

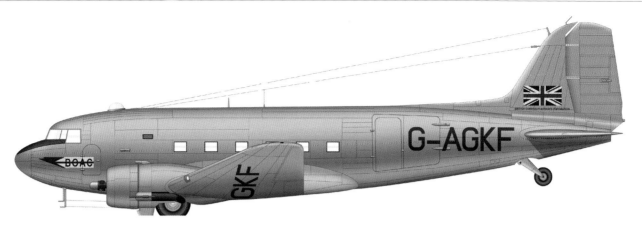

Another former RAF Dakota IV, G-AGKF was taken on charge by BOAC before being sold to the French commercial air company Air Nolis as F-BEFQ in September 1949. Its career was brief, as it crashed on 10 January 1950 and was written off.

Dakota G-AKNB was converted to civil configuration by Scottish Aviation in 1947 and served with Silver City Airways before being transferred to British United Airways Ltd in January 1962. In its later years it was one of the DC-3s converted to Basler BT-67 turboprop configuration.

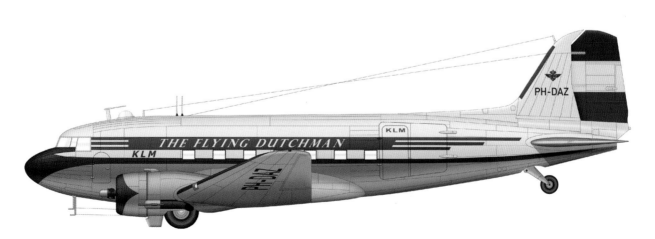

Dakota PH-DAZ was acquired by the Royal Netherlands Airline KLM in 1955. KLM was one of the earliest DC-3 customers prior to the outbreak of the Second World War, and used the versatile aircraft to re-establish its routes in the post-war years.

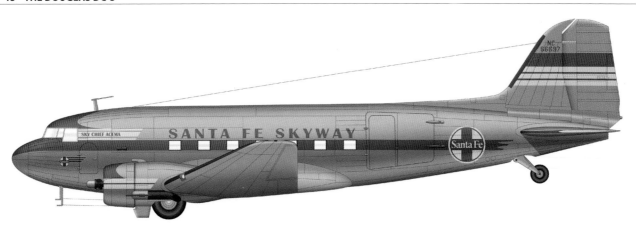

Santa Fe Skyway was one of the small airlines that took advantage of the flood of surplus military C-47s to open a commercial enterprise. Several such airlines operated Dakotas out of Santa Fe, New Mexico, in the 1950s and 1960s.

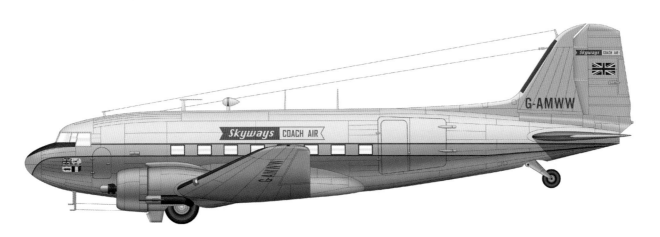

G-AMWW was built as a C-47B-30-DK at Oklahoma in January 1945, and taken on charge with the RAF as a Dakota IV in April with the serial KN492. In February 1950 it was bought by the Lancashire Aircraft Corporation and registered G-AMWW. In 1959 it was operated under lease by Air Charters of Ireland Ltd. It is pictured here in service with Skyways Coach Air in the 1960s.

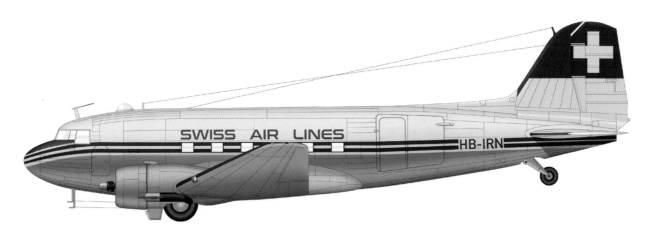

This Dakota served with the USAF as 44-77061, then the RAF as KN683. Sold to Swissair in 1947 as HB-IRN, it flew with that airline until 1964, before being allocated to the Swissair Aviation School until 1969. It was then donated to the Swiss Transport Museum in Lucerne, Switzerland, after being restored by the Swissair Fokker Team. It can still be seen there today.

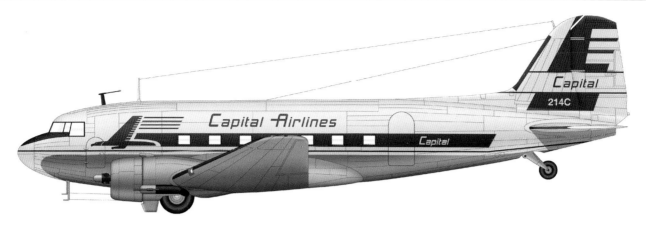

In 1948 Capital Airlines operated twenty-three DC-3s on its domestic routes, and introduced an economy class service called Coach Class to compete with the railroads between Chicago and New York City and the dominant airlines on the route: United, TWA and American. Each flight left at one in the morning and stopped for ten minutes at Pittsburgh (Allegheny County). The Chicago–New York fare was $29.60 plus 15 per cent federal tax; seats on all other flights cost $44.10 plus tax.

The DC-3 was a major milestone for Trans-Canada Airlines (TCA). It was used extensively on all domestic routes except over the Rocky Mountains. It flew as a companion to the faster Lockheed 14s and 18s and eventually with the Viscount which soon replaced it. TCA operated a total of thirty DC-3s. Twenty-seven were former C-47s and three were former USAF C-49s, all converted to airline configuration by Canadair. The first aircraft, CF-TDJ, entered service on 1 November 1945, flying between Toronto and New York. The final aircraft, CF-TEA departed on 13 April 1963.

OK-GAC of Ceskoslovenske Aerolinie was formerly a Russian Li-2, one of many sold as war surplus post-1945. After Czechoslovakia came under communist control in 1948, its national airline's western equipment was rapidly replaced by Soviet types, the Li-2s being supplanted in turn by Ilyushin Il-14 airliners.

Modelling the DC-3

Over the years the DC-3, and C-47, have been fairly well covered in modelling circles, mainly in 1/72 scale but gradually the other scales have started to catch up. But as both dedicated DC-3s were in service with civilian operators so were a growing number of former military C-47s after the Second World War. So before starting out on a model it is well worthwhile checking a few things that suit the particular model you are building. Engine intakes: Most DC-3s were fitted with the smaller ones but a few were fitted with the longer version more common on military C-47s.

Passenger door: Check that the aircraft had the dedicated passenger door and not the cargo door. Radomes and aerials: A quick check to see what variations go with the model you are building will avoid frustration down the line. These are small but important matters. Also, don't always just follow the decal instructions if you are using aftermarket decals. These days a quick search on the internet may well throw up photographs of the aircraft you are building. The slight variations are common and all over the place so a quick check goes a long way.

AIRFIX DC-3/C-47
(original tooling)
1/72 scale

The first Dakota kit in 1/72 scale was the original Airfix release from 1960. For many years this was the only game in town. Festooned with the well-known Airfix rivets, the kit was basic by today's standards but remained in their catalogue for many years.

The kit was typical of kits of that era: the engines were moulded into the cowlings and the surface detail was a mass of raised rivets. Cockpit detail was non-existent, with just two pilot figures that sat in an interior more akin to a pair of boxes. There was no passenger area detailing at all. The kit simply had the C-47-style cargo door, but did in fact feature three options for the engine nacelle intakes.

It was for many years the modeller's only option for a Dakota. As well as being issued in military markings, the kit was also put out in Silver City markings. In the early 1970s the kit was cleaned up and issued as a USAF AC-47 Gunship. This kit remained the Airfix Dakota until they issued the Italeri kit in their own boxing.

Looking back at the kit it is really nothing more than a kit of interest to collectors as it is now very long in the tooth.

AIRFIX DC-3/C-47
(new tooling)
1/72 scale

The new-tool Dakotas came from Airfix as part of their plans to gradually replace some of the older toolings. None was more welcome than the Dakota, which has been boxed in several variations. However, no purely civilian DC-3 variant is in their plans but even so the early smaller intakes are included on the sprues. There will be an aftermarket civilian door section released later in 2019 by Blackbird Models.

Moulded in the usual grey plastic with engraved detail, that some may say is a little too deep, the new kit has far more detail than any previous Dakota kits. The cockpit is well detailed and all you could really add are seatbelts although not a great deal can be seen once completed. The interior is fitted for military variants and not civilian seating. Have said that, not a great deal can be seen once the fuselage is closed up and the windows fitted. In fairness, an aftermarket set would be somewhat pointless as this would barely be seen.

One point worth making is that you must follow the kit instructions and also check the fit of parts before committing glue. Airfix have designed fine tolerances into all of their new kits and careless construction can lead to problems further down the line. Having said that, construction can go at quite a fast rate with this kit and it's not long before the fuselage is completed. I like how they have tackled the lower fuselage section which is in one piece. This gets around the problem that has often plagued previous Dakota kits with a somewhat flimsy joint between the wings and lower fuselage. Once this lower section is fitted, the kit really has a solid feel about it.

Careful assembly of the wings will minimize any joints and alignment issues. Tail surfaces are straightforward as are the engines. The two-piece cowlings fit snugly around the engines with just a slight joint to clean up. The windscreen needs to be treated with care as it can easily snap if you're too heavy handed with it. I found the upper and lower joint lines, where the windscreen fitted, needed a little trimming to get a good fit. A nice point is that the fuselage windows are added from the outside too. I would also suggest investing in a set of aftermarket canopy masks as these make life a lot easier. Overall the kit assembles quite quickly and only needs the odd little touch of filler on a few joint lines, quite often the fault of the modeller.

The kit I had featured two civilian Dakotas in the form of Dan Air and BOAC, the Dan Air being in the familiar Silver/White scheme while the BOAC was in standard RAF upper camouflage with Black undersides. These were used during the war with large civilian serials on the wings, in the hope they would not be considered a military target. In fact it was one of these aircraft that the actor Leslie Howard was aboard when it was shot down over the Bay of Biscay in 1943.

With all joints cleaned up, the kit was given a coat of primer before the surface was polished using a very fine sanding cloth. The upper surface was pre-shaded with Black along the panel lines before the dark Earth was applied. The camouflage was masked off using small rolls of White Tac and gaps were filled with Tamiya masking tape before the dark green was applied. This gave a subtle soft edge to the camouflage. After that the upper surfaces were masked off before the undersides were sprayed with Tamiya NATO Black. This is a very dark grey colour and not as harsh as normal black paint.

I added the undercarriage legs at this stage and these need a little care when adding the rear actuators to get them aligned. Once all was set, the entire model was gloss varnished and left overnight to dry out totally. I used the kit decals on the

build and these reacted well to decal setting solutions. I found that the large serials need a sharp blade running down the panel lines and a further dose of Micro Sol to get them to settle down snugly. It is advisable to leave the decals to dry out overnight.

Once this had been done, the kit was given a coat of gloss varnish to seal the decals before a wash of UMP Dark Dirt was applied. This dries in around thirty minutes and can be cleaned off using damp tissues. A little bit of exhaust staining was added using Alclad Transparent Smoke.

All that was left to add were the wheels, propellers and smaller items such as aerials, pitot tubes and the like. I use Vallejo Matt Varnish as this gives a nice even finish to the surface. Once dry, the masks were removed. And there was a completed BOAC Dakota.

The box on the left shows the original boxing of the first Airfix kit. As well as military markings ,the kit featured Silver City decals.

Below: The top box artwork for one of the releases of the new-tool Airfix kit.

The completed Airfix kit in BOAC markings as operated during the Second World War by the airline. It was an aircraft like this that actor Leslie Howard was killed in when it was shot down over the Bay of Biscay by a Luftwaffe Ju 88.

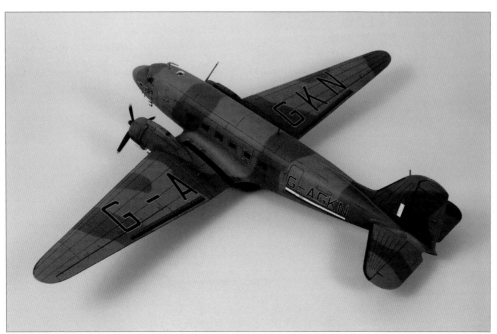

A view of the BOAC aircraft which was painted in RAF colours on the upper surface as well as the large civilian markings.

Above: The new tooling captures the sit of the Dakota very well indeed, including the weighted wheels.

Right: A rear view of the completed model.

Above: The kit features a well-detailed undercarriage as well as excellent engine and propeller detail.

Left: A view of the completed model.

The undersides of the BOAC aircraft were black. I used Tamiya NATO Black as it's not as black and gave a much better scale effect.

ESCI
1/72 scale

Released in the 1980s around the same time as the Italeri kit from the now-defunct ESCI model company of Italy, this was a kit issued in both military and civilian forms. Featuring engraved detail which seemed a little overdone, the kit was nicely moulded and included separate flaps across the lower wing. The civilian DC-3 boxing is the only 1/72 scale kit that features a full civilian seating arrangement.

Many thought the kit was the same as the Italeri one but there are a number of differences including the separate flaps and the level of engraved detail. The kit was reasonably simple to build but its one

weak point was the joint between the lower wings to lower fuselage which would need a strengthening strip added. Also, as with every other Dakota kit, the passenger door needs a little filling and rescribing to get a decent fit.

The kit featured a suitably detailed cockpit considering what can be seen on the completed model. And as stated before this is the only kit to feature full civilian seating in this scale. Apart from this, the model had a breakdown of parts very much like the Italeri kit.

The civilian variant came with decals for TWA- and Sabena-flown aircraft.

Although not been generally available for some years now, they can be picked up from auction sites.

ESCI issued a military and civil version of the Douglas DC-3. This old kit, released in the 1980s, can be still picked up on aution sites.

The kit is reasonably simple to build; its one weak point is the joint between the lower wings to the lower fuselage.

The diorama makes use of Bachmann railway figures.

The completed out-of-the-box ESCI build. Civil aircraft models are seldom seen weathered and derelict. Yet some DC-3s had such long service histories that weathering was inevitable, as was their final resting place in the corner of an airfield where decay would set in.

For the ESCI model I wanted to build a derelict Dakota. I opted to use different modelling techniques, not often used on airliners. I built the kit out of the box and didn't do a lot of added detail as this would be redundant on the finished model. The interior was sprayed grey and the basic construction completed. Considering the age of the kit, it went together quite well.

One thing I wanted to do was show the aircraft as left in an abandoned state and I so carefully removed the rudder. The rudder mounts were replaced with sections of plasticard. Also, I opted to leave the crew entry door open and build the model with all glazing removed. With the main windows it was simply a case of leaving them out of the build, but the cockpit glazing meant replacing the fuselage sections between each panel. This was done by using a small section of plastic strip, cut to size and added where the framework would normally be located.

I opted to leave one engine with the cowling removed too and have the tyres in a flattened state. I've never really been a diorama or figure modeller so hold my hands up to those who excel in this field but the aim was to show the modelling techniques usually used in military aircraft weathering that can be used in civil aircraft modelling. So often we see airliners looking like they have just rolled off the assembly line. These are working aircraft and so suffer a level of wear and tear that is often overlooked. The older airliners such as the Dakota have often been passed on to smaller airlines and haulage firms around the world, especially in Africa, Latin America and the like. Often these aircraft come to the end of the road and are abandoned on an airfield.

Once the basic construction had been completed, I gave the model a coat of primer, Halfords Grey, before polishing up the surface with fine polishing pads. As the metallic finish didn't need to be perfect, I used an aerosol can of silver to give me the basic finish. Once this had dried, I post-shaded the panels with Alclad Smoke before giving the model an overall thin coat of aluminium. This gave a good worn metallic look to the model.

On to weathering the model. After applying a wash using UMP's Dark Dirt, I used various shades of rust from Vallejo which were dabbed onto the upper fuselage and then streaked down the sides using a wide, flat brush. Building this up gradually gives the right effect. Have a practice on an old kit to get the hang of this technique. Also, a little of AK's Deep Brown wash was used on certain areas. This started to make the model look abandoned and left to the elements. Finally, a little dusting with Humbrol weathering powders finished it all off. The entire model was then given a light coat of matt varnish.

The base. Now admitting I've never been a big diorama modeller, I wanted a simple base for the model. This came in the shape of a simple black picture frame from Wilkos, the grass coming from a basic grass matt at the local model shop which was attached to the frame insert using white glue. Once dry, this was trimmed to fit and the base added to the frame. Before adding the model to the base, I produced

flattened tyres. The wheels were assembled and then the tyres flattened by pushing the wheels onto a heated knife. This gave just the right effect. The wheels were painted up and added.

Once complete, the model was attached to the base using two-part epoxy resin to give a strong bond. Then it was time to add smaller details such as vehicles and people.

I opted at including a Jeep and trailer which had been sitting around in a drawer for years. They were in an Academy boxing along with their P-51D Mustang. Both were built out of the box before being given a coat of olive green, followed by a wash and little dry brushing to highlight the detail.

The figures were simply picked up at my local model shop and were Bachmann factory workers. Along with where these were added, I decided to add a tarpaulin over the exposed engine and its cowling on the ground. These were produced by cutting a small square of kitchen roll which was soaked with varnish to help it settle down onto the kit parts. Once dry, these were painted olive green and dry brushed to bring out the detail and add some depth.

Above left: The tarpaulin, fashioned from a square of kitchen towel and varnished, and flattened tyres.

Above right: An Academy Jeep, along with the trailer used in the diorama, was taken from a P-51 kit.

Right: The tarpulin shaped over the uncovered engine. This DC-3 has been abandoned and left to the elements.

The kit's rudder was removed and the rudder mounts were replaced with plastic strip.

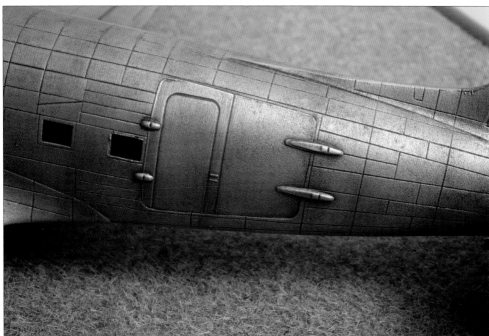

The entrance door shows the streaking technique used to give the model an abandoned appearance.

The completed model seen from the rear, in a grassy corner of airfield. The Academy trailer that accompanies the Jeep can be seen.

The Jeep used in the diorama was taken from an old Academy-51 Mustang kit. For 1/72 scale the Jeep is a very compact but detailed kit that suits the style of the diorama.

To show the abandoned look of the DC-3 the kit glazing was not used but the windscreen supports were added from plasticard strips. This gives the impression of broken or removed glazing from the finished model.

Another overall view showing the group of barrels which came from the railway modelling section at my local model shop. They were simply painted silver and given a wash to add some depth to them.

Flattened tyres. Rather than the usual weighted ones, I wanted to depict tyres on an aircraft that had sat derelict for a while. This was done by pushing the assembled wheels down onto a heated knife blade, but do take care if trying this technique.

Once the basic kit had been assembled and primed, the surface was polished then given a coat of silver from a rattle can. Once that had dried, I shaded the panel lines with black before applying a thinned-down coat of silver airbrushed on to give a worn look to the basic finish. This was all done before the weathering process could begin.

ITALERI
1/72 scale

Another 1980s kit, the Italeri one, has also been boxed in both civil and military guises and became the mainstay Dakota kit until the new Airfix tooling arrived on the scene. With somewhat finer engraved detail than the ESCI kit, this broke down in a similar fashion and was nicely detailed if not overdone. It only featured the military-style seating but once again when the fuselage was assembled very little could be seen of the interior anyway. Cockpit detailing was sufficient for what can be seen after assembly and again the cargo or passenger door would need a little filling and rescribing work.

The kit has been released several times with decals for varying civil operators as well as in its military guises. Construction follows the traditional method for kits such as this with the cockpit and cabin floor. This adds a little strength to the whole fuselage structure. As mine was based on a civilian aircraft, I opted to spray the interior light grey as opposed to USAAF interior green. With long, thinner fuselages I always use tube cement for a stronger bond, held together with masking tape and left to set completely. Kits like this require a little more patience but while the fuselage is setting, you can work on other areas.

The wing sections were assembled next and these left to set too. Before bringing both sections together, I added a piece of plasticard to the forward section of the lower fuselage to give the lower wing-to-fuselage section a stronger joint. This has always been a flimsy area in terms of Dakota kits.

Once complete, the joint lines were cleaned up and tail planes and engines added. Pretty soon the bulk of the construction was complete and the kit almost ready for paint.

I have always had a liking for unusual schemes and upon seeing the Kits World decals for the former Sabena aircraft that was put into service with Lufthansa during the Second World War, I was hooked. The interesting thing about the scheme was the yellow undersides with RLM02 Grey upper surfaces: not your usual airline scheme.

As it was a yellow underside, the model was first given a coat of white and very fine pre-shading before a couple of thin coats of yellow were applied. Once dry this was masked off before the RLM02 Grey was applied. The aircraft had black areas around the engine cowlings and nacelles which were painted in Tamiya NATO Black; pure black would not look right in this scale.

Once gloss-varnished, the decals were applied which went on superbly. Once dry they were sealed in place before the kit was given a dark dirt wash to bring out the panel detail. Slight exhaust stains were added before final assemblies.

A final coat of varnish sealed everything in and once the canopy masks were removed, the kit was all but complete. I hadn't fitted the kit windows into the fuselage sides but opted to use Krystal Kleer to fill them.

An overall view of the completed model showing the unusual Lufthansa scheme applied to the former KLM and Sabena DC-3s operated by the German airline during the Second World War.

Overall view of the kit finished in WW2 Lufthansa colours using decals from Kits World. Note the weathered look and yellow fuselage band, indicating a friendly or non-combat aircraft.

Above: Front end showing the silver propellers and engine detail which is not too bad considering the age of this kit. Until the new Airfix kit was released, this was the best on the market.

A view from above shows the upper surfaces in German RLM02 Grau. The engine nacelles were painted black in a similar style to the Ju 52 aircraft. Often it was done to hide leak and stain marks showing from the engines.

The undersides were in yellow which would have developed a very weathered look to it in a very short space of time. Also note the restrained exhaust staining too.

A side view of the model showing the civilian serial as well as the standard rudder markings applied to both civilian aircraft in German service at the time.

Another overall view of the completed model. Note the weathered look and yellow fuselage band, to indicate a friendly or non-combat aircraft.

MINICRAFT DC-3
1/144 scale

Dating back to the mid-1990s, this kit has been released in various boxings. It is a fairly simple kit albeit with a few errors along the way and silly little gaffs. My boxing featured decals for KLM among the options, in overall orange. The kit features engraved detail which is quite nicely done.

Construction is pretty straightforward and the bonus in this scale is that you don't have to worry too much about interior detailing. The kit has solid moulded side windows that are represented in decal form although the pilot's windows are in clear plastic. In order to keep some continuity I opted to paint these on.

Among the faults that have cropped up in reviews of this kit are that the tail is a touch on the small side, the cowlings are too long and the wheels oversize. To those you can add that the propellers would in effect catch the fuselage sides. But once assembled, the tail, cowlings and undercarriage don't look too bad. You can get round the propeller issue by the position you put the props in when adding them, so really you are getting round the issues without too much trouble.

The kit goes together without any real issues with just a slight clean-up of any joint lines. The wing-to-fuselage assembly is very straightforward with just a slight bit of trimming to get a good fit. The engine assembly is also very well done along with the undercarriage. In fact these types of kits go together very quickly indeed. The only area needing a little care is the lower wing-to-fuselage joint but this is nothing major.

At the painting stage I opted for the orange KLM aircraft as I like a scheme that is somewhat different. The Belgian DC-3s operated in this colour too but as a sign of neutrality. Later some were pushed into other uses. The other two options included are the Pan Am and Swissair schemes. The model was given a coat of grey primer which was polished using a fine sanding cloth. The smoother the surface, the smoother the paint finish. With orange being a somewhat horrible colour to paint, I first airbrushed a base coat of white.

After adding the base white, I masked off the pilot's windows before spraying them black. A gloss coat followed before decalling. I used the kit decals which acted far better than expected. Minicraft decals have not always been the best. The side windows came in decal form as well as the KLM markings. These were all sealed with a coat of gloss varnish before the model was given a wash of UMP Dark Dirt. Simply going on this colour it was obvious that the aircraft would have a worn look to it. The only other weathering was very slight exhaust staining.

Overall the Minicraft kit was a pleasant little build and despite silly errors does capture the right look of the DC-3.

The box-top artwork for the Minicraft kit showing the aircraft in Pan Am markings.

An overall view of the completed model in KLM markings. Alongside it is a pound coin to show the small size of the model.

An overall view showing the small size of the model from the opposite side.

A view of the completed model.

KLM aircraft were not fitted with the black de-icer boots to the leading edges of the wings and tail planes.

The kit is a fairly simple one to assemble without any major flaws to be wary of. The orange KLM markings making a big change from the usual silver ones. These were to highlight neutral civilian aircraft in times of war.

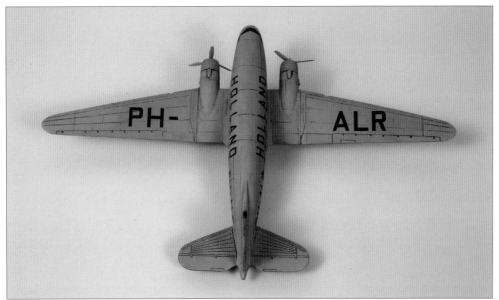

A close-up shot showing the undercarriage which is basic but fine in this scale. Also, the cockpit glazing was painted. It comes in clear plastic but I opted to paint these black to match the side windows.

A view from above showing the completed model. Considering Minicraft decals have not always had a good reputation, these performed superbly.

The fuselage windows were supplied in decal form. It seems that the fuselage serials are a fraction too big in comparison to photographs of the actual aircraft.

RODEN DC-3
1/144 scale

A more up-to-date kit came from Roden a few years ago. This Ukranian model company has been adding 1/144 scale airliners to their range for a while now and they make up into very nice models.

The DC-3 comes in green plastic with the usual clear sprues. All panel lines are engraved with restrained detail. As with most kits of this scale there is no interior detail, which makes sense as nothing could be seen. Assembly goes along very quickly with the fuselage and wings coming together in no time at all. I found a little bit of trimming was needed to get a good fit between the fuselage and wings, but not more than with any other kit.

The cockpit area comes as a separate piece which needed a touch of superglue and sanding down to get a smooth fit. As the model was going to be in natural metal, I added the engine assembly and undercarriage legs before painting.

After priming and attending to any joints that required sorting out, I polished the primer with a 3200 sanding cloth before giving the kit a coat of gloss black. Once this had dried, I gave the model a coat of Tamiya AS-12 Natural Metal which gives a great silver finish. A final coat of gloss varnish readied the kit for decals. The decals should be handled with care as they can tear easily but once in place they settled down quite well. The model was sealed with a coat of varnish before a wash was applied and some slight exhaust staining. This just left the smaller items to be added before a final coat of varnish to finish the model. As I hadn't used the kit windows these were filled with white glue. Overall a very nice kit and a bit of a step-up from the Minicraft.

The box top of the Roden kit showing the TWA scheme.

An overall view of the completed model in its silver finish. The trick with any silver finish is good preparation with primer and a gloss black base coat; then careful application of thin layers of silver.

Even with a smooth silver finish, a dark wash brings the panel detail to life. It helps give the model some depth to the finish.

Above: Another view of the completed model. The kit decals can be damaged if you don't apply them carefully as they are quite fragile.

Looking from above on such a small model, the TWA markings really break up the silver finish, something lacking in modern-day airliners.

The underside of the model is often overlooked by some modellers. Again, the wash brings it to life as well as slight exhaust staining too. But generally these aircraft were very well maintained.

TRUMPETER
1/48 scale

No dedicated civil Dakota has yet been produced in 1/48 scale, and it seems doubtful that one will be forthcoming in the near future. Two options are around: the old Monogram C-47 kit and the Trumpeter C-48C Skytrain. Chinese company Trumpeter have had a mixed time of things with their kits: some great choices with horrendous gaffs incorporated into their kits. A case of poor research and over-engineering make for awkward construction and frustration for the builder. I have to say their C-48 kit is typical of this.

The kit is for a C-48C Skytrain, which was a Pratt & Whitney-powered variant of the DC-3/C-47. It was initially operated in small numbers by the likes of United and Pan Am before many were pushed into military service with the USAAF.

The kit is a very comprehensive sight upon opening the box, with a high level of detail and engraved detail, especially rivets.

The cockpit is packed with detail which is worth careful painting as a fair amount can be seen on the completed model. There is a complete interior with seats, with detail right down to the etched brass seatbelts. Every possible item is included but sadly most of this will be invisible on the completed model. So I guess it comes down to what level of detailing you wish to pursue. I opted to leave the seatbelts out as the effort was not worthwhile. One problem with Trumpeter kits is that you don't always get good painting details for internals or smaller parts. Oddly, the kit instructions call for sky interior. Sky blue or grey? I opted for Tamiya sky grey as this seemed most likely. Seat cushions were painted brown and then highlights were picked out with dry-brushed light grey.

Care needs to be taken regarding the assembly of the interior or you may find issues when it comes to getting the fuselage halves together. So always be aware of making sure you line everything up correctly. The glazing needs to be added before the fuselage halves come together as does the tail wheel assembly. I found that the interior needs lining up well before putting the fuselage halves together, again using tube cement for a strong bond.

While the fuselage halves were setting, I turned to the wing assembly where the main halves go together easily with locating spars included. The central wing section requires the assembly of the undercarriage bays and engine assemblies including. The mounts

Below: The box art for the Trumpeter C-48 kit.

Bottom: The Trumpeter kit features real rubber tyres in the kit along with a choice of plastic or metal undercarriage legs.

for the engines between two bulkheads is a nightmare to line up. It cannot be seen on the completed model but is over-engineered rather than being produced for easier assembly. This was time consuming as well as a very frustrating part of the build.

Once this was completed, the central section and the fuselage could be brought together. I found this wasn't the greatest of fits and any slight errors seem to magnify as sub-assemblies came together. The wing-to-fuselage joint needed a fair bit of fettling and filling to get a decent fit. The outer wing sections slotted into place with just a smear of filler.

With all the hassle during assembly it wasn't a model I enjoyed, which often seems to be the case with Trumpeter: superb or flawed. It fell into the latter category for me.

Once the major assembly had been finished, I applied the Eduard canopy masks before giving the kit a coat of primer. As the kit was released as a military C-48C there were USAAC decals included and civilian decals for this aircraft were few and far between. The kit includes only the later longer intakes above the engine nacelles which restricted decal options even further. After a while I came across an Arctic Decals sheet for an aircraft operated by Karhumaki Airways in Finland during the 1950s and opted for them.

I polished the primer finish with a sanding cloth before misting on the first coat of silver. For this I used Halfords Mini Super Silver which gave a great finish. A couple more coats gave me the right kind of finish for the model. Once it had set, the fabric areas were painted with dull aluminium, before starting on the white upper fuselage. This aircraft has a demarcation line that has a step in it, so to ease the masking I

A rear-view shot of the completed model with the weathered look that suited the operating conditions the real aircraft would have flown in.

A close-up view of the forward part of the kit. The engine cowlings were a very poor fit considering the over-engineered feel to the kit.

copied the decals onto paper using my scanner. This allowed me to mask off the right size and shape before applying the white upper fuselage colour.

The model was gloss varnished after the de-icer boots had been masked off. And this was left 24 hours to cure fully. The Arctic decals are ink-jet printed and need care to apply. The black sheet was fine but the one with the red cheat lines and lettering needed a coat of Micro-scale Decal Solution to seal and protect it. They also need careful handling when applying so if you are using any decals like this, take your time.

The decals all went on without a real drama but as they were designed for the old Monogram kit the windows didn't match up 100 per cent, so a little touch-up work

was needed. Once the decals had dried out overnight, the kit was given a coat of varnish to seal everything in before any weathering was started.

The kit was given a dark dirt wash and exhaust staining, giving it that well-used look, which seemed fair considering the conditions it would have operated in. Once this was completed, the final assembly was done with things such as the propellers, aerials and undercarriage. The kit offers the option of metal undercarriage legs as well as rubber tyres. A final coat of matt varnish dulled it all down and the masks were removed.

I have to say this wasn't the most pleasurable build I have ever done. I was simply glad to see the back it.

An underside view showing the good level of detail. However, the engines and cowlings are not a great fit.

Looking down onto the finished model showing the extent of weathering applied with a panel wash and other amounts of staining.

Above: The Trumpeter kit features real rubber tyres along with a choice of plastic or metal undercarriage legs.

An overall view of the finished model.

A view of the rear port fuselage showing the passenger door and rivet detail.

Aftermarket Items

This is by no means an exhaustive list and represents products available at the time of going to press.

Conversions (1/72)

Alley Cat Models:

AC72032C Dakota	Basla BT-67 Turbo Conversion

Flightpath:

FHP72200	Wright Cyclone Engines

Transport Wings:

TWC72015	Dart Dakota
TWC72016	Dakota Glider

Decals (1/144)

Arctic Decals:

ARC144001	Karhumaki Airways/ Kar Air
ARC144002	Aero Oy/Finnair

Flying Colors:

FC44017	Piedmont
FC44041	Northeast

Lima Oscar:

LD44010	LOT
LD44012	Air France

LPS:

LPS14417	Classic Air
LPS14418	BEA
LPS14426	KLM
LPS14434	Panair do Brasil

Decals (1/72)

26 Decals:

72-53	Ethiopian Airways
72-145	Intra Airways
72-146	Intra Jersey
72-147	THY Turk Hava Yollari
72-193	Air Anglia
72-110	Air Atlantique 50th Anniversary

Arctic Decals:

ARC72005A	Karhumaki Airways/ Kar Air
ARC72005B	Karhumaki Airways/ Kar Air
ARC72012A	Aero Oy/Finnair
ARC72012B	Aero Oy/Finnair Early
ARC72012C	Aero Oy/Finnair Late
ARC72077	Airveteran

Blue Rider:

BR2102	Aeroflot

Kora:

KORD72317	Lufthansa

Kits World:

KW762122	Sabena
KW72127	Lufthansa, BOAC

LPS:

LPS72002	Panair do Brasil

Techmod:

TM71147	LOT

TM72148	LOT

Thunderbird Models:

TBM72009	Trans Canada

Transport Wings:

TWF72003	Rhodesian Air Services
TWF72007	Central African Airways 1956
TWF72008	Central African Airways 1962
TWF72009	Central African Airways 1966
TWF72010	South African Airways 1956
TWF72011	South African Airways 1962
TWF72017	Hunting Clan Airways 1959
TWL72002	BEA Pionair 1952
TWL72003	Derby Airways 1962
TWL72004	KLM 1964
TWL72005	Sabena 1965
TWL72007	All Nippon Airways 1960
TWL72008	Ozark Airlines 2006
TWL72009	Qantas Airlines 1960
TWL72010	Silver City Airways 1959
TWL72011	Trans Australia Airways 1960
TWL72012	Varig 1965
TWL72020	Ansett 1958
TWL72022	Capital Airlines 1955
TWL72024	Eagle Airways 1956

Decals (1/48)

26 Decals:

48-12	Intra Jersey

Arctic Decals:

ARC48001	Karhumaki Airways
ARC48002	Kar Air
ARC48003	Aero Oy/Finnair Early
ARC48004	Aero Oy/Finnair Late
ARC48019	Airveteran

Max Decals:

MAX4806	Aer Lingus

Techmod:

TM48100	LOT
TM48101	LOT

Multi Scale Decals: printed to order

F-Decal:	Air France, Flugfelag Islands, Sabena, Thai Airways

Other Accessories

1/144

Armory:

ARAW144001	Dakota Wheels

Peewit:

PEE144044	Canopy Masks (Roden)

1/72

Airwaves:

AEC72190	Etched Brass Detail Set (Italeri)

Armory:

ARAW72011	Dakota Wheels

Blackbird Models:

BMA72033	Dakota Airliner Door (Airfix)

Eduard Brassin:

ED672046	Dakota Wheels

Eduard:

ED72252	Dakota Detail Set (Airfix)

Peewit:

PEE72076	Canopy Masks (Airfix)

Pmask:

PK72101	Canopy Masks (Airfix)

Quickboost:

QB72051	Dakota Engines (Italeri/Revell)
QB72490	Dakota Engines (Airfix)

Scale Aircraft Conversions:

SAC72023	Metal Undercarriage Legs (Italeri/Revell)
SAC72089A	Metal Undercarriage Legs (Airfix)

Thunderbird Models:

TBM010	Canopy Masks (Airfix)

1/48

Aires:

AIRE484446	Dakota Wheels (Trumpeter)

Eduard:

ED48607	Etched Metal Landing Flaps (Trumpeter)

Montex:

MXMM48290	Canopy and Insignia Masks (Trumpeter)
MXSM48290	Canopy Masks (Trumpeter)

Quickboost:

QB48081	Dakota Engines (Monogram/Revell)
QB48238	Dakota Rudder (Trumpeter)
QB48329	Dakota Corrected Engine Cowlings (Trumpeter)

Scale Aircraft Conversions:

SAC48009	Metal Undercarriage Legs (Monogram/ Revell)

Trumpeter 1/48 DC-3 C48C

Well, it has to be said that Trumpeter's offering of the DC-3 is an interesting topic in 1/48. The kit comes with a full interior and engine details across seventeen sprues. The first impression you get is how detailed the kit is. The construction is pretty straightforward with the interior being nicely rendered, and the crew areas in particular being beautifully represented.

I'm not sure if I had a 'Friday' moulding, because when it came to enclosing the cabin plate into the fuselage, the fun really began. It would be fair to say the fuselage fought me all the way. This was a real pity, as up to that point construction was going smoothly. Eventually the two halves met, in a fashion, and a little bit of filler was used too.

The one thing I did notice as I test-fitted the two halves was how dark the interior was, so I left the curtains out as the glazing is quite thick and I wanted as much natural light to shine into the cabin. The wings fitted together beautifully with

some wonderful mouldings, which were sadly let down by the clumsy rendition of the leading-edge lights.

Mating the wings and fuselage transforms the model and earlier frustrations were well rewarded. I chose to paint the DC-3 in the colours of Aer Lingus, and was lucky enough to source some Max Decals of a couple of versions of DC-3 that Aer Lingus used mid-twentieth century. I also took the opportunity to do some online research regarding colours, finish and configuration. All seemed to change over time so I settled for a happy medium and set to painting.

Whilst the smaller decals in Max Decals kit were of good quality, the larger stripes were very brittle and quite possibly measured for the Monogram DC-3 kit. As such, a little refresh with the paintbrush was required to sort out the snags.

Overall, a good kit, but beware of fit issues, poor painting guide and occasionally confusing instructions.

Single seats were lined up on the production line with one side of the buckles fitted. The plastic seat sides helped keep the buckles in place once glued. Each seat received a quick rub-over with some 1200 grit wet and dry to sort out the mould seam lines, ready for painting. A small amount of Gator's Grip Thin Blend PE glue was applied in preparation for the PE strap. The seamlines are cleverly hidden by the chair side.

Start of the Pratt & Whitney Twin Wasp engines. Beautifully detailed but some awkward seamlines.

Test fit the rear set of cylinders to the exhaust manifold. For some reason this set was a little tighter than the subsequent fitting. Here the second row of cylinders has been added. Note the ignition leads moulded into place. Here the seam lines are highly visible, especially on the cylinder heads. These are moved with some folded sandpaper, whilst the body seamline is cut away.

Double chairs are shown prior to a final clean-up with 1500 grit wet and dry before priming. The seatbelts are in position and make a great focal point for the kit.

All seats in place, with belts and a wash of dark green to bring out the depth of their surface. I went for a green in keeping with the Aer Lingus corporate identity.

I built the engine as a whole unit thus the propeller boss was glued into position in the final drive cover using a rod to ensure it was centred. With the push rod and final drive cover in place, I was ready to start cleaning up the engine in preparation for painting. As the push rod assembly was delicate, I found that easing it into position with a knife blade was the best way to avoid breakages.

Twin Wasp mounted up ready for installation into its nacelle. The engine mounting plate bearers are fiddly, so take your time. A final clean before priming and we're in business.

The centres of the Aries resin wheels were drilled out ready for the axle. I drilled from both sides to ensure the bore was straight with a 3-mm bit. Both wheels were detached from the moulding block and cleaned up. No bubbling or blow-outs in the casting. Note the slight bulge where the tyre meets the ground. A beautiful touch.

Here the wheels are mounted to the white metal landing gear main struts that come with the kit – strong enough to hold the main body of the aircraft.

A matt black base coat was applied to both Twin Wasp engines ready for painting. The engines were painted using a mix of Citadel and Tamiya paints and washes and were treated to a dry brush of Citadel Mithril Silver. The propeller shaft cover was given a coat of Citadel Blue Grey while the cam rod was given a coat of Chaos Black. The propeller shaft cover was then given a coat of Citadel Spacewolf Grey, which received a wash of Chaos Black to add some grime. The ignition power leads were brought to life with Tamiya XF9, Hull Red and the propeller cover was washed with Burnt Umber. The exhaust manifold was treated to a thick wash of DecoArt Soft Suede to simulate heat damage. The mounting base received a coat of Mithril Silver followed by a black and then a burnt umber wash. The compressor got a coat of Citadel Chainmail followed by a wash of Chaos Black. Don't worry about the odd bit of paint missing the intended area. This won't be seen once the undercarriage gear is mounted. Finally, the compressor received some detailing paint and the whole wheel bay was given a wash of dark green.

The white metal main landing gear strut needed a bit of work to remove the casting seams, but some time with the files sorted that out. Here the multimedia undercarriage is complete. Note the position of the head of the side struts on the base of the main landing gear. It is also a good idea to use the undercarriage as a jig to ensure the landing gear struts are mounted straight and true.

The rear tail wheel was finished in Citadel Chainmail and given a light wash of black while the suspension piston shafts (circled) were finished with Mithril Silver. The tyre was painted with Tamiya NATO Black.

The main landing gear wheels were painted with Tamiya NATO Black and given a black wash to highlight the details of the treads. Note the flat bottoms.

The interior of the wheel wells: note the position of the U-shaped support band. This isn't well shown in the instructions and took a little bit of research to locate its true position.

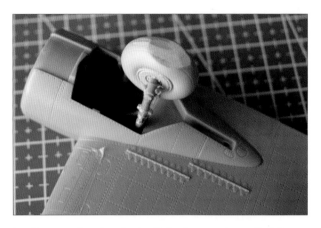

Landing gear placed in wheel wells for the next phase of building, using the wing as a jig.

The compressor was given a coat of Citadel Chainmail. This was followed by a wash of Chaos Black. Don't worry about the odd bit of paint missing the intended area as it won't be seen once the undercarriage gear is mounted. If it is, it's weathering. The compressor then received some detailing paint and the whole wheel bay was given a wash of dark green and a final wash of burnt umber before the wheel bay was finished.

Right: The crew areas on the opposite side of the cabin.

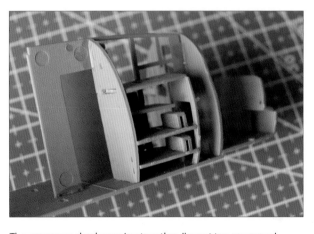

The crew areas slowly coming together. I'm not too concerned about the sink marks as they're out of sight once the model is constructed.

The cockpit instruments are from Eduard's C-47 update set. Note colours of the handles in the centre console and various avionics kit in the crew area. The floor of the cockpit is given a wash of burnt umber to bring out its crisp details. The rudder pedals are washed with a black wash.

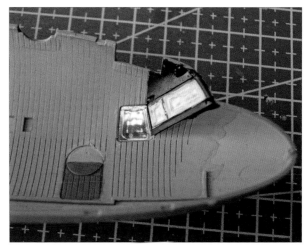

The cockpit coming together. The crew door is in place and the windows fit nicely in their respective apertures. My only complaint is that the plastic used is rather thick.

Crew seating area, showing extinguishers. The bench seat is finished in Vallejo German Cam Pale Brown 70825. The area within the circle is an overhead light which is painted silver on the reverse.

One of the pilot's seats ready for installation. The Eduard coloured etch harness really brings this item to life, so is well worth the effort.

The propellers were given a coat of matt black, the blades were then painted Chaos Black, the boss was finished in Boltgun metal and the protecting cover Mithril Silver.

The pilot's seat in situ with the Eduard self-adhesive instrument panel. The adhesive isn't the strongest so I reinforced the panel with Gator Glue.

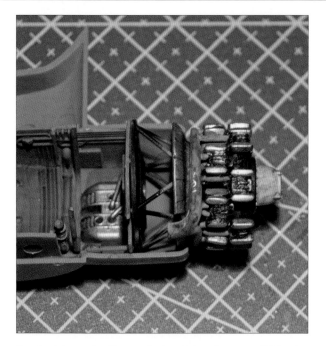

Test fit of the engine. The weathering of the exhaust manifold and wheel bay make the model stand out.

Right: The whole wing was checked for fit prior to gluing. The elastic bands kept the top sections of the engine housing and wheel bay with the lower wing in place while the glue cured.

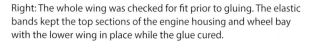

Sadly the Quickboost cowlings were too short. Notice the blown-out bubbles in the casting. These would be filled prior to painting if used.

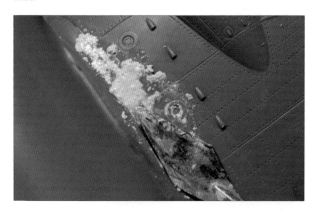

The gap between the wing and the fuselage needed some attention so Milliput was dampened and, using a palette knife, pushed into the gap.

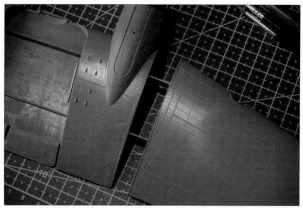

The wing fit is spot on. Trumpeter have really thought about the this element of the kit.

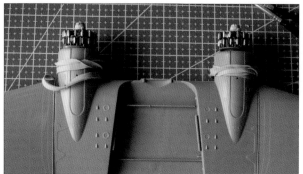

As this is a civilian version some elements aren't used. The aperture on the exhaust shroud was filled with stretched sprue cut to fit. It was glued into place with liquid cement. Once the stub had dried, it was removed and sanded with 1500 grit wet and dry.

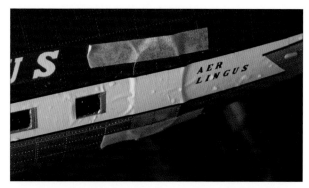

The passenger door was held in place while the decals were laid over it. Sadly, the longer decals were extremely delicate and had to be cut into sections after tears were noted during wetting.

On looking at contemporary photos from the 1950s, I noticed Aer Lingus DC-3s were missing the astrodome and large light panel above the cockpit. These were filled with plasticard. The blue sheen on the windows is Vallejo latex mask.

The wing lights were given a coat of Citadel Chainmail, while the lights were painted Mithril Silver and varnished with a coat of Aircraft Colours Gloss Clear before the clear plastic was added.

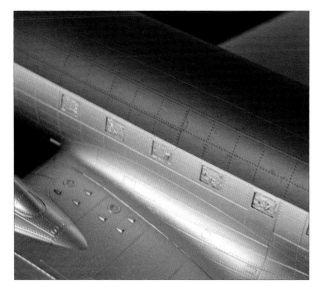

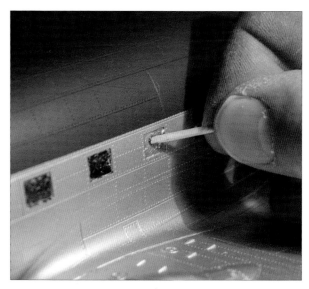

The whole model was given a coat of acrylic floor polish which gives the matt deep green a wonderful satin sheen. The fuselage was then ready for decals.

After the polish had dried, the liquid mask was removed from the windows with a sharpened cocktail stick. The windows then received a coat of window cleaner to remove the remaining traces of masking.

Test fit of the wheels and propellers.